MAP

OF THE GROUNDS OF THE

REHOBOTH BEACH

Camp Meeting Association.

William B. Wiggins Surveyor

REVEALING REHOBOTH: AN INSIDER'S GUIDE

By Neil Shister
With Molly MacMillan

Design Director Rob Waters

Published in the United States by Mulberry Street Press, LLC
Washington, D.C.

Mulberry Street Press
4711 Rodman Street, NW
Washington, DC 20016
www.MulberryStreetPress.com

First Edition: July 4, 2014

ISBN: 978-0-9835969-3-6

Print and Bound in the United States of America

TO ORDER COPIES
www.RevealingRehoboth.com

REVEALING
REHOBOTH

An Insider's Guide

By Neil Shister
with Molly MacMillan

Rob Waters, Design Director

Photography by
David Koster, Molly MacMillan
Rob Waters and Bob Yesbek

Special Thanks to Rehoboth Beach Historical Society

The Mulberry Street Collective

Mulberry Street Press

TABLE OF CONTENTS

CONVERSATION: SAM COOPER
Mayor of Rehoboth

'WHAT MAKES REHOBOTH SPECIAL ARE COMMON VALUES'

Rehoboth chooses a Mayor every three years and in 2014, for the 9th consecutive time, 685 of 1077 voters who went to the polls (out of a total registration of 1384), elected Sam Cooper. A fourth-generation local, Sam Cooper has participated in the city's governance for more than three decades (beginning as a Councilman in 1981) and witnessed close-hand its on-going evolutions.

"My great grandfather was a farmer who came into the area, to Old Landings near Rehoboth, and carved a farm out of the woods. My grandfather moved into town. He was a contractor, had a sawmill, and got up shipwrecks. I still live in the house he built.

I have always lived in Rehoboth. In 1970, I was in the first class that graduated from Cape Henlopen High, which was consolidated from separate schools in Rehoboth, Lewes, and Milton. Then I went to Indiana for college but I got homesick and left after the first quarter. Let's say I always had a lot more ability than motivation as a student. Later, I enrolled at Del Tech where I studied civil engineering.

People talk a lot now about Rehoboth becoming a 'year-round town' but it will never be the year-round town I grew up in. We had three movies, bowling alleys, two pharmacies, three barbershops, an A&P grocery store right at First Street and Rehoboth Avenue. There was one school, about 500 kids in grades one through twelve.

It was a year-round town but layered on top of it was the summer business. Sussex County is real rural and Rehoboth came with the mindset of a rural place but it was different from the rest of the county because we had this influx every summer of people who had money and were sophisticated. We got to mix with them.

Then the real estate values became great, too great for the locals so they migrated out of town to live. Now it's more the people from outside Rehoboth who patronize the restaurants and bars. Many of the in-town houses are rentals or investment properties, not full-time residences.

What makes Rehoboth special are our common values. We put a lot of emphasis on its small town nature, that's in our Comprehensive Development Plan. Ocean City used to have a downtown that was a lot like Rehoboth, then they decided to go all out for tourism, whatever it took! The problem we always have in government is getting people to buy in to being part of the overall whole. Zoning and the regulatory side of city government is where this can get nasty. Houses used to cover 50 percent of the lot, now they max-out the building envelope up to the edge of what's allowed. I like to say that 'years ago people built within the zoning code, now they build right up to it.'

The other big thing here is trees, you're not going to find this many trees close to the ocean anywhere along the east coast. But when people max out the size of their house, there's not a lot of trees left. Or, with the smaller lots, the trees get cut down to build a new house.

You can talk about trees and buildings, but in the end it's the people that make a place. You set yourself up with a certain character and hope that it attracts a certain folk who become invested in that vision and want to preserve it. Come to Rehoboth and hopefully you feel like you're part of a small town that you can be immersed in, you're almost a local if you want to be. That's a different experience than, say, a theme park where everything is put on to attract your money. ■

• •

"Rehoboth Beach is now and will remain a town within a town. It has two sets of active users—residents and visitors. It has two physical identities—residential community and resort. Maintaining balance among these various identities is a continuing challenge of managing traffic, parking, oceanfront land use, municipal services, business stability, commercial and neighborhood appearance, and governance."

Rehoboth Beach Comprehensive Development Plan, 2010

INTRODUCTION
A REHOBOTH STATE OF MIND

To fully appreciate Rehoboth Beach, one begins with the recognition that it is as much a state of mind as a physical place. Which is not to minimize that this is a beautiful spot with the spacious beachfront, wooded glens extending right to the shore, and two fresh water lakes. But it is Rehoboth's promise that provides the magic, the deep-seated faith that here there is just the right mixture to make most any dream possible.

Take its nickname, 'The Nation's Summer Capital.' No act of Congress was needed to stamp this official, just some commercial chutzpah and a willingness to suspend disbelief! To a remarkable degree, Rehoboth Beach is what you want to make it.

In mood and personality, Rehoboth Beach harkens back to an earlier, simpler time. Unlike today, with vacations meted out in miserly week intervals, Rehoboth came of age in an era when families uprooted to the seaside for the entire season. That legacy of leisurely indolence is etched deeply into the local DNA. Unlike most every other spot along the Atlantic, Rehoboth remains a quintessential turn-of-the-1900s beach town right down to the caramel popcorn and saltwater taffy. Sure, it's grown bigger and more year-round, but its character is still languid by nature.

Things Rehoboth stem from the same fundamental starting point: the allure of the water, the fresh resin smell of pines, and a temporary reprieve from 'real life'. All that's required to savor its splendor is the willingness to embrace (for Type A over-achievers, the apt verb might be 'surrender to') the rhythms of its dawdling, sun-drenched, laid-back tempo.

The saving grace for this way of life is that it's not just for the rich. To be sure, DuPonts (and their friends) summered here in houses that belied their grandeur (or at least square footage) by being called 'cottages'. That's carried through to the present, the median value of homes nestled in the leafy enclave of Henlopen Acres (population 122) exceeds $1 million making it perhaps the richest spot in Delaware. Even so, much of what makes Rehoboth special can still be had on a budget.

Take the tale of Harvey Waltersdorf for example. The Rehoboth Museum has gathered an extensive collection of oral histories to preserve the town's legacy, one of which is with Harvey Waltersdorf who first came to Rehoboth as a young boy in 1936. "We started out with a tent over in Shaw Park (now called Grove Park), Wilbur Shaw had given the property to the city for people who couldn't afford hotels and they

would camp here all summer. Mother always reserved the spot next to the guard shack because it had a faucet right outside, you didn't have to carry water as far if you were going to have coffee or tea or wash your dishes." Shaw Park was a Delaware boy's version of Huckleberry Finn's life on the Mississippi. "We had a pier down there to the canal, you could crab. There were pot-luck dinners in the big screened-in pavilion. Everybody would bring something; if the men were out fishing we'd all have fish that night. It didn't really cost much because you didn't have much money, you made do with what you had."

There's another equally important component that shapes the Rehoboth Experience, a kind of counter-weight to nostalgia, the ying to its yang. Call it 'drive.' Amidst the distrac-

SHAW PARK CAMPING, Circa: 1930s

tions of high season, it's easy to miss this less conspicuous side to Rehoboth that might best be described as 'the pursuit of the ideal'.

Whether presented as refined (if casually understated) elegance or camouflaged as high kitsch, there is considerable ambition here to convert dreams into reality. To stand out. To raise standards. To contribute. To improve. Sometimes it's directed toward the self, sometimes towards the community; it can be cultural or gastronomic or aesthetic or even commercial. Regardless of the specific focus, there is a discernible undercurrent to the local vibe that encourages residents to make their personal contribution toward improving the town's quality of life. This has led to

the creation of the likes of CAMP Rehoboth, the Rehoboth Jazz Festival, the Rehoboth Film Festival, the Rehoboth Art League, and Clear Space Theater

Right from its start, Rehoboth Beach has been a community pursuing an idealized perfection.

Not counting the native Americans from the Delmarva hinterland who came here for seasonal repose (leaving behind archeological mounds of discarded oyster shells that are periodically discovered in Cape Henlopen State Park), the town began in the mid-19th century with revivalist Methodists from Wilmington. Led by Reverend Robert Todd, who had envisioned in a dream a seashore retreat in a site much like Rehoboth ("And the Sea

CITY OF REHOBOTH BEACH

On January 27, 1873, the "Rehoboth Beach Camp Meeting Association of the Methodist Episcopal Church" was incorporated by the Delaware legislature for the purpose of establishing "a permanent camp meeting ground and Christian sea-side resort." With the coming of the railroad in 1878, the growth of the community was accelerated. On March 19, 1891, an act was passed incorporating the municipality as Cape Henlopen City. The name was formally changed to Rehoboth in 1893. Since its founding the City of Rehoboth Beach has continued to be one of the most popular resorts on the Atlantic coast, attracting thousands of visitors each year.

S-90

Hath Spoken" was the title of his sermon), a camp meeting association dedicated toward the cleansing of souls and renewal of faith was established in 1873. No card playing, no dancing, no alcohol. A decade later the association disbanded (the temptation of walking to nearby Dewey Beach for a drink may have been its undoing), but not before a number of small one-room wooden structures (called 'tents') had been built. The dye was cast. Within a few years, the real estate developers arrived and have never left.

Since then, Rehoboth Beach has been on the map as a summer get-away (Victorian architecture can be spotted downtown).

Rehoboth is no longer a spiritual outpost; the pilgrims who now come are drawn largely by hedonistic pursuits. They're here as much to restore the body as to purify the soul. Even amongst the most secular, though, there's still an itching for improvement and betterment. Perhaps it's something in the drinking water that makes people become impatient here with their 'same old same old' selves. There is an impulse to break with convention, to try on something new.

Like entering the ocean, which according to an early promotion for Rehoboth Beach once seemed daunting without instruction: "Don't stand shivering and shrinking back from the spent waves. Walk briskly out until waist deep and sink down

until the water touches your chin …You are not an accomplished bather until you have learned to float. Lie down quietly on your back in the water. Be perfectly still and fearless, you won't sink unless you commence to struggle. The art is simply doing nothing with a vengeance."

Memorial Day weekend, when 'No Left Turn' signs appear on Rehoboth Avenue, is a kind of sacrament of renewal. There are few who would think of it this way, but each time Rehoboth re-opens for the summer it offers abundant promises of possibility from something as grand as a new lease on life (or love) to lesser ambitions like stopping to smell the roses.

We wrote *Revealing Rehoboth* to help first-time visitors (and long time residents, as well) better enjoy and participate in this special place that consistently ranks among America's favorite vacation spots. Amongst gay folks, Rehoboth has become a celebrated destination, a stopping point on the Grand Tour that includes Provincetown and Key West. Regardless of gender, the pleasures of the place abound. No less an authority than *National Geographic* rates the old-school wooden boardwalk as one of the country's top ten.

Dozens of good (and sometimes great) restaurants have made the town a destination for foodies (from *haut gourmet* to on-

going debates about the best pizza or French fries). The bumper cars of Playland are legendary. Crowds and traffic in August may be in intense, but a stroll around Lake Gerar is to enter a sylvan glade akin to what Shakespeare might have imagined in *Midsummer's Night Dream*. And of course there's the shopping along Route 1, multiple outlets offering well-financed brands at (sort of) discount prices.

"Crazy and tony at the same time," is how *Fodor's Guide* describes Rehoboth. That sums up perfectly this incongruous blend of beach town and classy get-away. Most anything you want you can get in Rehoboth Beach and, if you want nothing more than to be left alone, that can be had here, too.

In his book *Rehoboth Beach Memoirs*, James D. Meehan perhaps summed up best the cocktail of experience that constitutes Rehoboth. "Of all the resorts on the Atlantic Coast, there is none quite like Rehoboth Beach ... It has that indefinable magic quality that makes certain places special. It's sophisticated but friendly; exciting but not intimidating; relaxing but never boring."

What Mr. Meehan wrote in the year 2000 is perhaps even truer today. ∎

By Neil Shister

REHOBOTH BEACH HISTORY

English explorers, probing the Virginia coastline for a westward passage to India in the early 1600s, gave name to Rehoboth Bay.

They took their inspiration from the ancient Hebrew word for 'broad place,' the spot where the sons of Abraham finally established a foothold in the Euphrates valley of the Philistines. Here the Isrealites finally were able to secure water (their previous wells had been destroyed by hostile locals). "And Isaac called the name of the well Rehoboth," reads Genesis 26, "and he said 'for now the Lord has made room for us and we shall be fruitful in the land.' "

THE VISIT OF THE PIRATE CAPTAIN KIDD

Never was there a pirate more (in)famous than Captain William Kidd, whose penchant for burying plunder in isolated spots inspired the novel Treasure Island. So bad was he that, after being hanged in 1701, Kidd's corpse was left to dangle in a metal cage over the River Thames in London as a warning to others.

In 1699, Kidd piloted the San Antonio into the calm waters of Indian River Bay. With his ship heavily laden and sitting so low in the shallow water that it was endanger of running aground, Kidd dropped anchor.

So legend goes, to lighten the ship he ordered that four chests be filled with East Indies treasure: gold from China, rubies, sapphires, and uncut diamonds. These were loaded onto a longboat, which he and several oarsmen paddled to shore. The chests were lowered into a six-foot hole dug at the base of a large, single oak tree. A diamond shape was etched into the bark and a cannonball placed atop the filled hole.

Several weeks later, Kidd put into port in Boston and was arrested. He was sent back to London. Within a year he was 'gibbeted,' hanged in chains and left on display. He died never disclosing the location of the buried treasure near Rehoboth.

The story was well known along

The Gibbeting of Captain Kidd

the Delaware coast. Indeed, the site of the first grand house in the area, now the home of the Rehoboth Art League in Henlopen Acres, may have been situated so the owner could hunt for the buried chests. In 1743, when Peter Marsh built his homestead, it was considered quite odd to locate so near the water. Few residents did so, because of the mosquitoes and the toxic effect of salt air on plants. Local legend had it, though, that Marsh could be often spotted on the dunes, hunting for Kidd's treasure. ■

The land proximate to Rehoboth bay, low ridges of sand hills, had been inhabited for some 10,000 years. When the Europeans arrived, several native tribes populated it. The Lanape, commonly called the Delaware because their territory flanked the river, would migrate in the face of expanding white encroachment, going as far north as Canada. Smaller groups——the Nanticoke ("Tidewater people") and the Assateagues (whose nearby barrier island is now known for wild horses)——largely disappeared.

Historians believe these native Americans were seasonal visitors to the coast, coming here annually from further in-land to establish summer camps where they could feast on an abundance of fish, clams and oysters and crabs, turtles, ducks, and wildfowl.

Farmers started arriving near the turn of the 1700s, entitled by land grants emanating from the Duke of York who sought to defend control of southern Delaware from attack by rival Marylanders, as occurred in 1673 when they burned Lewes to the ground.

The leading citizen amongst these new settlers was Captain John Avery, who moved from Maryland in 1675 to establish a homestead that would eventually encompass hundreds of acres on the north shore of Rehoboth Bay. A seafarer and master of the sloop Prosperous that sailed between Maryland and Barbados, after retiring to his Delaware plantation he continued to serve as a Captain of the local militia. William Penn commissioned him Sussex County justice of the peace.

Avery's home site was identified in the 1970's by a surface survey as a probable archeological site. Among the items was a silver Spanish Piece of Eight, coins were few in this region where tobacco was the primary currency of exchange.

If a single factor changed Rehoboth from coastal dunes into a more established settlement, it may well have been oysters. So suggests Michael Morgan, author of the definitive *Rehoboth Beach: A History of Surf and Sand*. Oysters were prized fare in America, their ubiquity in various forms described by one foreign visitor as "pickled, stewed, baked, roasted, fried, and scalloped … fresh as the fresh air, and almost as abundant." Those from Rehoboth Bay were considered among the best, so much so that by the 1850s the Delaware legislature had banned oystering from May through August to protect the beds from depletion. Industrious watermen had bestowed

Greeting the Train, circa 1900

upon Rehoboth what Morgan calls "its first taste of renown."

But it would not be until after the Civil War that Rehoboth Bay gave birth to Rehoboth Beach, "summer retreat and bathing place." The Rev. Robert W. Todd of Wilmington, so the tale goes, weary from weeks of presiding at Wilmington tent meetings in the summer of 1872, went off to retreat on the New Jersey shore. It did the trick. In the weeks that followed, the idea of establishing a "Christian seashore for the Delaware peninsula" consumed him. Little more than a year later, in 1873, his evangelism bore fruit. The Methodist Episcopal Church created the Rehoboth Beach Camp Meeting Association (after first considering naming their grounds Atlantic Beach) and bought some 400 acres from two local farmers for around $10,000 at a spot called Rehoboth Neck.

The camp plot fanned out from the camp grove (at what is now Gove Park) in a wedge intended to offer all landowners an unobstructed sight-line to the sea. The community's main thoroughfare, Rehoboth Avenue, ran from the grove to the water's edge. It would be described in a subsequent development prospectus as "three-fourths of a mile in length, one hundred feet wide at the grove, designed to be one of the grandest avenues in the world."

Over a thousand residential lots were for sale to Camp Meeting members, at $50 each (specifically priced to be more affordable than those on the Jersey Shore). Small, narrow wooden cottages were built, called "tents," most no more than two rooms without heat, electricity or indoor plumbing. Meals were prepared in the grove meeting area and eaten communally.

The by-laws governing residents were strict, befitting a community where recreation focused on a tabernacle that could seat 500 people. Dancing and card playing were disdained. Alcohol was forbidden, the nearest place to get a drink was a mile south of town on the Dewey line.

Todd's experiment with an austere retreat of the pious proved short-lived. People were more drawn to the pleasures of the shore than Methodist rigors, dooming the religious nature of the resort. In 1879, 'Camp Meeting' was dropped from the name of the Rehoboth Beach Association; two years later the meetings themselves were discontinued.

It was around then that the Junction and Breakwater Railroad extended its freight line from Lewes south to Rehoboth Beach. The train would open up Rehoboth Beach to Washington and Baltimore vacationers, and later even Philadelphia. Originally the tracks stopped at the camp meeting ground but, as the influx of visitors grew (some arriving in their own private parlor car), the station was moved to within a block of the shore. (In 1987 the historic station would be transported via flatbed truck to its present location at 502 Rehoboth Avenue, where it now serves as the Chamber of Commerce Visitors Welcome Center).

The town, at that point incorporated as Cape Henlopen City, hired its first municipal employees in the 1890s: a policeman (whose main duty was capturing stray animals), a surfman to serve as a life guard, and a lamplighter for the gas lights (the position was for the summer only, from 6 p.m. through 11 p.m.) who also who trash collector. A speed limit on city streets of six miles per hour was established. The first mayor was elected in 1903.

Stately cottages lined the boardwalk. As did Hill's Bath House, constructed by the Chief of Police after a number of male bathers, arrested for swimming without clothes, blamed their public exposure on the lack of a suitable place to change clothes. Cows roamed freely until a city ordinance prohibited them from the ocean block of Rehoboth Avenue. Frazer's Lake, (across from the Henlopen Acres yacht basin) was the site of watermelon parties and rowing outings until its waters were drained into the Lewes-Rehoboth Canal. In 1922 Rehoboth had 690 residents in winter, 4500 in the summer.

To more sophisticated eyes, the unique charm of Rehoboth was apparent. Mrs. Henry B. Thompson of Wilmington, built a 'cottage' here (her other getaway was in Bar Harbor, Maine) and recalled her first impressions:

"The dunes with their soft covering of marsh

The Canal Bridge, circa 1940s

grass, the wonderful aroma of the pines soothing us to a restful sleep, the birds, the flowers, the bay. Particularly the moonlight. All were like balm to the weary."

Equally apparent to Mrs. Thompson, though, were Rehoboth's limitations.

"The little town was very shabby on first crossing the canal. At the left, a forlorn tumbled down old skeleton of a building came into view, surrounded by briar, weeds, etc. The main avenue ending at the glorious sea was cut in two by the Pennsylvania Railroad tracks, a shabby station and unsightly comfort stations. In front of the Hotel Henlopen was a dump … I did not feel that Rehoboth was doing herself justice."

Just as the railroad transformed Rehoboth Beach, even more so did the completion of the road from Georgetown in 1925. Within a decade, real estate development was booming and summer residence had tripled to 18,000. Rehoboth Heights became part of the town in 1926, the same year in which Irenee DuPont agreed to dredge and clean Lake Gerar and stabilize the town's banks in return for permission to sub-divide lots, realign streets, and receive certain abandoned rights-of-way for personal use. He sold lots to friends with the understanding that they would preserve the surrounding woodlands.

Streets were paved in town. A connector was built to Dewey Beach. Going to the post office and walking the boardwalk replaced meeting the train as the principal social event of the day. Celebrities were occasionally spotted.

Despite proximity to the water, neither commercial fishing nor shipbuilding was important in Rehoboth. The biggest enterprise in town was the Stokely cannery, which began operations in 1928 on the west end of the Lewes-Rehoboth Canal, a location chosen to enable produce to be shipped

THE REV. ROBERT W. TODD

Delaware-born in 1831, the Rev. Robert W. Todd received a Doctorate of Divinity from Dickinson College and served as minister to various Methodist churches throughout his career.

He described his boyhood schooldays in a recollection: "The school-master was a new arrival in the neighborhood. The house was really a deserted negro cabin, that stood by the highway side, three miles from Denton. For an area of twenty-five square miles between that town and the Delaware line, this was the only school... The entire curriculum of our school was covered by the three cabalistic letters, R., R., R., understood to represent the three great sciences, Readin', Ritin' and 'Rithmetic. The three G's, Grammer, Geography and Geometry, had then scarcely been dreamed of as ever possible to be taught in a country school."

His death in May, 1906 was noted by a memorial in The Christian Advocate:

"...Brother Todd was a man of marked personality. Nature had endowed him with a gracious combination of qualities. He was a rare conversationalist, sunny, affable, and informing; a counselor with wise ability to advise.

FOUNDER OF THE REHOBOTH BEACH CAMP MEETING ASSOCIATION

He was a confident, prayerful, Bible-loving and joyous Christian, and, although interested in all the recent phases of theologic unrest, his faith rode serenely at anchor in the old verities. His preaching was fluent, reverent, magnetic, and sometimes rapturous.

God had given him a voice, mellow and persuasive song power, which he used with great effectiveness in his work. He literally sang the gospel. It was his weapon against doubt and fear." ■

USS REHOBOTH

The first *Rehoboth* was built in 1912 as a fishing vessel in the Milford shipyards of W.G. Abbott and commissioned as a U.S. Navy patrol vessel in 1917. For a mere six months she patrolled the coast of France, until her hull developed an unstoppable leak (the construction of trawlers turned out to be entirely unsuited for hard seas). The crew was taken off and a British cruiser sank her.

There was also, incidentally, a USS *City of Lewes* that similarly started life as a menhaden trawler built in the Abbott yards; she spent most of her time as a minesweeper.

The second *USS Rehoboth* was built as a seaplane tender (support vessels that operated long-range reconnaissance seaplanes from harbors). In service from 1944 to 1947, she was refitted in 1948 as an oceanographic survey ship. Her mission was to sail to uncharted areas of the seas to retrieve specimens of the ocean bottom, measure ocean temperature, and take samples of seawater at different depths. In this capacity, the *Rehoboth* discovered an underwater mountain range in the Atlantic with heights up to 12,000 feet and, in 1953, became the first ship to anchor in water deeper than two-and-one-half miles.

After more than a decade's service in the Pacific, she was decommissioned and sold for scrap in 1970.

in by barge. Local peas, stringless beans, beets, tomatoes, and lima beans were all canned here. Tomato puree was transported out via a railroad spur to the Campbell Soup Company in Camden, New Jersey.

On the eve of World War II, one local resident would observe that Rehoboth Beach "… offered all the warmth of a country village in the winter and became a very cosmopolitan community in the summer." An element of cosmopolitanism during the 1930s, according to local legend, was a brothel that operated for a decade at Fourth and Sussex. It was run by a couple named Mary and Barney who drove a Lincoln touring car, attracting a clientele from New York, Wilmington, and Philadelphia that reputedly included a number of prominent men.

In 1937, by virtue of public referendum, the Town of Rehoboth was re-named "City of Rehoboth Beach." An official airfield was opened the next year, with flights between Rehoboth and the airport near Washington in College Park, Maryland (it would close in 1986).

German U-boat submarines posed a real if under-reported threat throughout World War II. About 90 percent of the nation's oil refining capacity was near Wilmington at the start of the war and passed through Delaware Bay, making for a prime strategic target. Tales abound of people standing on the boardwalk watching ships on fire at sea. The fear of spies and saboteurs was high. Checkpoints to monitor cars were set up north and south of Rehoboth, the boardwalk was off-limits after dark. Coastal artillery was installed at Fort Miles to defend the coast, with observers positioned in tall watchtowers to look for enemy warships. Mounted Coast Guard horseback patrols policed the beach.

The spanning of the Chesapeake Bay Bridge in 1954 further transformed Rehoboth, opening up the shore to explosive real estate development as the beaches became much more accessible. As more Washingtonians arrived, the biggest celebrity would be Vice-President Richard Nixon and family, the town began calling itself 'the nation's summer capital.'

Summer folk wanted vacation rentals, investors were eager to provide them. The real estate business boomed. Malls started appearing along Route One (Midway shopping plaza was the first, opening the same year as the Bridge). The great hotels were razed, their lots sub-divided. Most of the vestiges of small town life—a local movie theater, pharmacy, hardware store, homey restaurants—would disappear in the wake of the new land boom. The town high school, which first offered a complete curriculum in 1928, was absorbed to form centralized Cape Henlopen High

THE HOUSE OF PROSTITUTION

"When I first came to Rehoboth, I stayed with my younger sister on Fourth Street. This house of prostitution, of course the people in Rehoboth called it a whorehouse, was next door to my sister. It was a nice big brick house. We sat on the porch and watched the local men, who left through the front entrance. Which was quite interesting. One happened to be the mayor of Rehoboth at that time … The man and the woman came from Wilmington and they brought these girls with them. We never did see the girls leave on their own, like take a walk or go down the beach, or do any of those things. Whenever they left, the left in the nice car with the woman, who was married".

Mrs. Dorothy Truitt

● ● ● ● ● ● ● ● ● ● ● ● ● ● ● ● ● ●

"We would come home from the beach, got a shower, and got into something fit to walk uptown with for the early evening —-cotton dresses and white shoes. We would walk the length of the boardwalk. Both the Henlopen and the Belhaven had orchestras that played there. The Henlopen had rather formal dances on Saturday nights, women wore long dresses and high heels."

Mrs. Betty Raughley
Barnes, circa. 1920s

BEAUTY QUEENS

Legend holds that the first Miss USA Pageant in history occurred in Rehoboth Beach in 1880, with Thomas Edison serving as a judge. Not all agree. Skeptics say it is unlikely the Methodist establishment would have sanctioned such a thing (and that the only convention held in Delaware that year was the state's teacher association).

Rehoboth Convention Hall was home to the Miss Delaware pageant for forty years, from 1966 until 2006 when the venue shifted to Dover Downs. During that period two local Rehoboth girls won, Kathleen Atanassi in 1974 who would have a longtime career as principal harpist at Walt Disney World, and Nancy Lynn Ball in 1984, a jazz dancer who went on to tour with the Miss America Showstopper Troope that year.

in 1970 (along with students from Milton and Lewes); the Seahawks, once the pride of Rehoboth (a restaurant offered free meals when they won the 'big game' against Lewes) were no more.

Pizza showed up in1960 when Dominick Pullieri and brother Joe modestly opened what would grow into an institution, Grotto Pizza. "Most people were not familiar with pizza," Pullieri recalled. They had to pass out samples on the sidewalk that first summer to create a market. For want of a more historic moment, the 'coming of pizza' can be said to mark the beginning of Rehoboth's modern era.

Some twenty years later, a second gastronomic event marked another social threshold. Throughout the 1970s, two disco dance clubs, The Renegade and the Boathouse, were drawing gay visitors to town. At the end of the decade two restaurateurs, one gay and one straight, opened the Back Porch and then Blue Moon; Rehoboth was on its way to becoming a first-class eating town.

In its current iteration, Rehoboth Beach has drawn from the foundations of its past and the vitality of its present to emerge as a trend-setter. The residential up-scale that began with Henlopen Acres has spread, producing neighborhoods of handsome houses that have avoided the numbing 'square foot over-kill' of other beach towns. A renaissance is in bloom as the town comes out of the Great Recession of 2008. Commerce is trending up, with stylish and original shops. A slew of ambitious chefs and restaurateurs have established a dining district that itself has become a destination.

The AARP calls Rehoboth one of five 'dream towns' for retirement (nearly 40 percent of the population is over 65) with its combination of low cost living (no sales taxes, low property taxes) and high-interest activities (ranging from the Sea Witch Festival to the Art League, the Film Society with its annual festival, and classical Coastal Concerts). Environmentalism is alive and well, exemplified by the work of the Delaware Center for the Inland Bays. There is hopeful talk of building a pier on the canal to enable water taxi service to Lewes.

Rehoboth has become a model of enlightened diversity, guided by the pioneering leadership of CAMP (Create A More Positive) Rehoboth in integrating the gay and straight populations. Indeed, Rehoboth Beach today occupies a prominent place within gay America, ranking alongside Provincetown, Key West, and Fire Island on the east coast chic circuit.

"Rehoboth Beach is now and will remain," reads the Comprehensive Development Plan certified by the state in 2010, "a town within a town. It has two sets of active users—-residents and visitors. It has two physical identifies—-residential community and resort. Maintaining balance among these various identities is a continuing challenge of managing traffic, oceanfront land use, commercial and neighborhood appearance, and governance." ∎

REHOBOTH BEACH
HISTORICAL SOCIETY MUSEUM

Founded in 1975, the mission of the Rehoboth Historical Society is to preserve and showcase artifacts that illustrate the development of the community.

The Rehoboth Beach Historical Museum, opened in 2007, works toward that end with a permanent collection and rotating exhibitions. Housed in what was the town's landmark icehouse at the entrance to town on Rehoboth Avenue, the Museum is something of a a hidden gem.

Unlike many a dusty small-town repository of nostalgia, the Rehoboth Museum exudes vitality with its deftly mounted permanent and rotating exhibitions. "Exceeds expectations" is the frequent response from visitors, "everything about it is top notch and high quality."

Permanent displays illustrate the evolution of the community, spanning the earliest days of Rehoboth's native Nanticoke people 12,000 years ago to the old Cape Henlopen Lighthouse and the grand hotels of the glory days. Lots of vintage photographs hang on the walls. Particularly interesting is a display of the multi-layer regalia that constituted a woman's bathing attire, in the early 1900s, that typically weighed thirty pounds soaking wet (no wonder swimmers of that era took such pains not to lose their footing in the surf, it was tough to get back up).

New shows are constantly being mounted to refresh the collection which, in prior years, have included a potpourri of subjects such as Sand Pails, World War II in Rehoboth Beach, Beach Eats, and 'Surfing, Skimming, and Floating Off the Delaware Coast.' ∎

511 Rehoboth Avenue
(302) 227-7310

Ample free parking

CONVERSATION: NANCY ALEXANDER
Director, Rehoboth Beach Historical Museum

courtesy of Carolyn Watson Photography

Nancy Alexander, Director at the Rehoboth Beach Historical Museum since 2007, grew up in a small beach town in New York where her uncle was Mayor.

"Some two decades ago, I applied for a job at the Rehoboth Art League (in college I had started an after-school arts program for kids at the campus museum). I arrived for my interview at night, having never before been to Rehoboth Beach. When I woke up the next morning and walked down the street, I fell in the love with the place. It felt like home, I was back in my childhood. Even if I didn't get the job, I knew I'd come back. I got the position, and met my future husband on the first day of work.

The Historical Museum is due to Warren MacDonald. The City had bought the old icehouse and he was the first to envision it as a museum. Warren kept working the idea until it happened. We lease the building from the City for $1 a year, although Mayor Sam Cooper made us pay $50 in advance!

I tell people I have the best job in the world, I get to study 'the history of fun at the beach.'

If I were explaining what makes Rehoboth special, I'd say 'look at the amenities that the Camp Meeting folks created and left behind to make this the perfect resort community: wide avenues down the middle of town, lots of trees, the first beautiful boardwalk.' I'd also point out the uniqueness of the geography. Once you cross the canal, there are two fresh water lakes and stands of pines that go very close to the ocean. The other thing is the atmosphere here. Vacationers return for decades, generation after generation, bringing with them vivid memories. A lot of places don't have that continuity.

The core mission of the museum is to gather and interpret our collections, which range from signs for arcade games to photographs and post cards. You cannot begin to characterize it. When the SS Tracy wrecked on the beach, for example, a high school resident hacked off a piece of the propeller and mounted it on a board; we have it. Things that people might not think are important—-a photo, a restaurant receipt, an old trinket tucked away—-all have a story to tell.

I'd say the single best piece we have is the original plot map of the town drawn for the Association. We also have a group of remarkable photographs from glass-plate negatives taken in 1906. The clarity of the details is just astounding.

Our challenge is to interpret these 'ordinary' things for people who didn't grow up here. Like the high school football trophy on display. You have to know the back-story to appreciate it. On Thanksgiving Day, there would be an annual game between Rehoboth Beach and Lewes. It was a big deal! We have the trophy from the final game before the two schools were consolidated into Cape Henlopen High.

What would I like most have in the collection? The Dolle's sign would be nice to have in the building, but that's not going to happen." ∎

STATISTICAL PROFILE OF REHOBOTH BEACH:
YEAR-ROUND RESIDENTS

POPULATION (2012): 1,373 a decrease of 8.2% from 2000 Census;
Median Resident Age: 59.1

POPULATION RACIAL BACKGROUND: White alone (94.7%); Hispanic (3.6%);
Asian alone (0.7%), Black alone (0.5%); Native American (0.2%)
ANCESTRIES: English (19.0%), German (18.8%), Irish (15.7%), Italian (7.4%), French (4.0%),
Scottish (3.8%);
ESTIMATED MEDIAN HOUSEHOLD INCOME: $77,457 (from $51,429
in 2000);
ESTIMATED PER CAPITA INCOME: $62,670;
ESTIMATED HOUSE OR CONDO VALUE: $813,511 (from $296,000 in 2000);

LIKELY HOMOSEXUAL HOUSEHOLDS (counted as self-reported same-sex unmarried-partner households): Lesbian couples: 2.6% of all households
Gay men: 6.8% of all households

#7 on the list of "Top 101 cities with the largest percentage of likely homosexual households (counted as self-reported same-sex unmarried-partner households)

AVERAGE HOUSEHOLD SIZE: Rehoboth Beach: 1.7 people
Delaware: 2.5 people

PERCENTAGE OF FAMILY HOUSEHOLD:Rehoboth Beach: 41%
Delaware: 67.4%

PERCENTAGE OF HOUSEHOLDS WITH UNMARRIED PARTNERS:
Rehoboth Beach: 10.9%   Delaware: 7.3%

REHOBOTH BEACH COMPARED TO DELAWARE STATE AVERAGE:
Median house value significantly above state average;
Unemployed percentage below state average;
Black race population percentage significantly below state average;
Hispanic race population percentage below state average;
Median age significantly above state average;
Foreign-born population percentage significantly below state average;
Percentage of population with a bachelor's degree or higher significantly above state average;

source: City-Data.com

BEACH
& BAY

THE OCEAN

The nearness of the sea to the inland bays, within walking distance in some spots, makes Rehoboth Beach a very special place to experience the water. Only narrow barriers of land separate the two, co-joined by the rhythms of the tides that flow in and out through the Indian River Inlet.

"The Atlantic Ocean," writes author Simon Winchester in his magisterial book *Atlantic*, "is surely a living thing. It is forever roaring, thundering, boiling, crashing, swelling, lapping. It is easy to imagine it trying to draw breath where it encounters land, its waters sifting up and down a gravel beach, it mimics nearly perfectly the steady inspirations and exhalations of a living creature."

Rehoboth Beach has always been an ideal spot to savor this living, pulsing presence. Indeed, the attraction of the ocean here has always been as much of an object of inspiration as recreation. It wasn't until the 1900s, with Rehoboth already firmly established as a summer retreat, that swimming became popular and most people actually went into the water.

There is no natural harbor here for boating, commercial fishing has never been important. Water temperature ranges from the mid to upper 50's in late May to a high of around 70 degrees Fahrenheit in late August Although open to the sea, Rehoboth Beach does not attract big waves and is typically free of dangerous 'shorebreaks' where waves break directly on the beach. The ocean current along this stretch, in contrast to most of the east coast, runs south to north until it collides with Cape Henlopen. To get the full effect of heavy surf, one must go Herring Point in Cape Henlopen State Park up the beach (too far by foot!). Through most of the summer, Rehoboth beach waves measure one to three feet, with

courtesy of Portraits In the Sand

the highest surf occurring in August and September due to tropical weather patterns. Fierce winter Nor'easters have recorded eight-foot high waves.

Beach replenishment is a constant practice, both by dredging off-shore slurry and pumping it in as fill, and through protective measures like erecting dune fences and planting dune grass. In the wake of Hurricane Sandy, the Corps of Army Engineers began a major project in 2013 budgeted at some $37 million to reduce the effect of flood and coastal storm damage from the northern end of Rehoboth Beach to the southern end of Dewey Beach. This is a follow-up to similar projects performed in 1998 and 2006 that more than doubled the size of the beach.

Compared to other resorts in Delmarva, however, erosion to Rehoboth Beach has been relatively slight. The beach has natural protection because of its unusually high elevation (23 feet) and the series of groins that trap sand. As one expert says, Rehoboth is a "beach that rebuilds well."

Even so, waves breaking at an angle transmit part of their energy along the shoreline, which transports sand and leads to erosion. Rehoboth's bulkheads and groins, rigid structures of steel, timber, and stone built perpendicular into the water, were first constructed in 1915 to protect the beach and slow this long shore drift. There are now thirteen of them. The problem with groins is that, while sand is deposited on the up-side drift where it widens the beach, the ocean current moves faster on the downside of the groin, which actually accelerates erosion.

"If that ocean has very little resistance to go through before it gets to the boardwalk, the roads and the hotels behind are imperiled," explains a Delaware Shoreline and Waterway Manager. "So it's the recreational and storm protection values that make it vital we do these projects." ■

POODLE BEACH
QUEEN AND PROSPECT STREETS

Poodle Beach, located just south of where the boardwalk ends, is the prime Rehoboth Beach gathering spot for 'beautiful boys and masculine men.' This place to see and be seen was named by *USA Today* as one of America's Best Gay Beaches.

The high point of the beach social calendar is the traditional Drag Volley Ball Game on the Sunday of Labor Day weekend, an event that draws hundreds of spectators both gay and straight (and even got national attention on *The Today Show*). The game typically starts at 1:00 p.m. but *cognoscenti* know to arrive early to get close to the court.

The origins of the name Poodle Beach, which came into vogue in the late 1970s, are hazy. One theory holds that two cousins would drive up in their Cadillac and make camp on the beach accompanied by their poodle dogs. Another explanation says it's because the spot attracted so many gay guys all coiffed and groomed like poodles.

Prior to becoming Poodle Beach, this stretch of sand was known as Carpenter Beach, in homage to the branch of the DuPonts who had nearby houses. Louisa Carpenter was perhaps the best known of this clan, celebrated for appearing at social occasions dressed in men's suits and ties and entertaining the likes of Greta Garbo and Tallulah Bankhead.

Hundreds of gays flocking to Poodle Beach were often less than welcomed by this entrenched Old Guard, who thought of the shore as their private domain. In 1978, the Washington *Blade* reported incidents of eggs and water balloons being tossed at the bathers from the dunes of the Carpenter enclave. A legendary encounter ensued when several men stormed up to the house to contest their rights to the beach. "Darling," a middle-aged blonde haired lady reputedly responded, "it comes down to 'haves' and 'have nots.' We are the haves and you are nots." ∎

A BEACH PRIMER

RULES AND REGULATIONS

• Red Flags indicate the area in which beach-goers are permitted to swim.

• The following are prohibited on the Beach and Boardwalk: Alcohol, Glass Containers, Feeding the Seagulls, Skimboards, Swimming to-and-from a boat (violators will be fined!)

• Bicycles and Rollerblades after 10 a.m. (May 15- September 15)

• Dogs are prohibited from the Rehoboth beach and boardwalk at all times from May 1 through September 30, but are allowed on the beach in Dewey Beach (just south of the RB Boardwalk) before 9:30am and after 5:30pm. They must still be on a leash and have a Dewey Beach Dog License. Dogs are allowed in the state parks.

'RED ALERT'

JELLYFISH: Very common off the beaches of Delaware, the highest concentration is found in August and September. Most jellyfish are non-stinging and can be ignored.

If you are stung, follow these recommendations to help alleviate the pain (which usually lasts 10-15 minutes): Do Not Rub, Rinse with Fresh Water, Apply Ice or Baking Soda to soothe.

SHOREBREAKS: This is a condition when waves break directly on the beach. Shore waves are unpredictable and dangerous. They have caused many serious neck and spinal injuries to both experienced and inexperienced bodysurfers and swimmers. Remember, small waves can be dangerous, too.

RIP CURRENTS: Often called undertows, rip currents are more prevalent after storms and form when water rushes out to sea in a narrow path, typically caused by a break in a near shore sandbar. Telltale signs are a difference in the water color (murkier or darker) and foam moving steadily outward.

Escaping from Rip Current

Rip currents, extending as far out as 1000 feet and travelling at speeds of three milers per hour, can pull even experienced swimmers away from shore.

If caught in a rip current, don't panic or swim against the current. Rather, swim parallel to shore until you are out of the current (they are rarely more than 30 feet wide). If you can't break out of the current, float calmly until it dissipates, usually just beyond the breakers.

DELAWARE STATE SEASHORE PARK

Just south of Rehoboth and Dewey Beach on Route One stretches an untouched maritime environment, which includes six miles of a wide swath of sparkling sandy beaches along the Atlantic Ocean. Inland on the Bay side lies miles of pristine tidal wetlands that shelter a biodiversity of wafting sea grasses, native fish, shell creatures, and flocks of migrating sea birds.

The Delaware State Seashore Park encompasses the entirety of this natural playground and has set up a number of facilities for the public's use.

A good place to gain information about the park is the Indian River Life-Saving Station Museum and Gift Shop. Here you will find a centralized resource for all of the park's scheduled events and facilities. There are weekly summer programs with registration at the Life-Saving Station Gift Shop.

For history buffs, there is an annual Maritime History Festival with a reenactment of an actual breeches buoy rescue by active-duty Coast Guardsmen firing a Lyle Gun. Usually every Friday there is a guided tour of the Life-Saving Station Museum and the nearby Coast Guard Station, where you can compare the ship rescues of today with those of yesterday. For those who like more personal detail, the Museum offers a look at the Surfmen of the U.S. Life-Saving Service and how they were idolized in pop-culture around the turn of the twentieth century.

On Friday afternoons there is a nature hike across the Inlet Bridge where a guide explains the impact of the Inlet on the history of the Delaware coast as well as present day changes in the coastline. There are other nature-themed events during the week, which include stargazing at night, a wild crab chase, seining the Bay, and several eco-tours by pontoon boat and kayak. To see the full calendar of events go to www.destateparks.com or call (302) 227-6991.

There are two guarded swimming beaches at Tower Ocean Road and the South Inlet Day Area, 9am-5pm. Parking fee is $4 resident/$8 non-resident for the day. There are also two designated board-surfing areas at Tower Ocean Road and the North Inlet breakwater.

For those who enjoy seeing the beach on horseback, there is a parking area at Key Box Road for trailers during the year when horseback riding on the beach is permissible. Check the website for times and locations. There is also Four Wheel Drive access to the beach at Key Box Road, Conquest Entrance, and 3R's near Beach Cove on the South Inlet. These sites are equipped with air pump stations and all vehicles must have a surf-fishing vehicle tag.

The State Park has extensive camping and RV facilities located at the South Inlet. Reservations are required, book early because sites go fast.

Indian River Marina is a full service boat dock with 274 wet slips and 156 dry stack slots. There is also a public use boat ramp. ∎

By Robert Sturgeon

COIN BEACH

400 barrels containing British half pennies and gold rose guineas were lost in the 1785 shipwreck of the Philadelphia-bound *Faithful Steward* near the Indian River Inlet. In the 200 years since, thousands of finds have given the stretch of Delaware Seashore State Park just above the inlet the name "Coin Beach".

CAPE HENLOPEN BEACHES

The beaches at Cape Henlopen State Park are worthy of high praise, indeed. The undeveloped beachfront, some six miles long from the Rehoboth entrance at Gordon's Pond to the Delaware Bay at Lewes, is lined with dunes (including the towering Great Dune from which the big guns of Fort Miles looked out during World War II).

It may be local pride, perhaps, but there are those who compare the surf scape here with Cape Cod (which, like Henlopen, is a cape scooped out by a south-to-north current).

Thousands of visitors are attracted to the beaches of Cape Henlopen. Indeed, on the busiest days—4th of July, Memorial Day—the gates to the park are often closed because of too many people.

North Beach is commonly referred to as 'Bathhouse Beach' because of its changing rooms and showers. With abundant parking, a bare-bones concession stand, and a functional walkway down to the sand, it is the park's principal swimming beach. Life guards patrol the waters in season.

Herring Point offers a more rugged beach experience (here is where the surfers hang out alongside a stone jetty to catch breakers). No life guards here.

Point Comfort Station provides a cross-over where vehicles licensed to fish can drive onto the sand. The strip is less populated here than more crowded North Beach, although swimmers must sometimes dodge fishing lines. ■

DELAWARE CENTER FOR THE INLAND BAYS

Established in 1994, the Delaware Center for the Inland Bays is an outgrowth of the federal Clean Water Act which established a program to monitor the environmental health of estuaries and oversee the implementation of conservation measures. The Inland bays include three interconnected bodies of water: Rehoboth Bay, Indian River Bay, and Little Assawoman Bay.

The Center engages in research activities and habitat protections, as well as educational outreach. Since inception, the Center has invested nearly $1.5 million in research ranging from continuous monitoring of bay health indicators, to the investigation of individual solutions to pollution like specialized cover crops on farm fields. The Center serves as a key link in the research process by helping to communicate results so that the public, resource managers, and elected officials can put them to work.

The Center is perhaps best known for the preserve it manages at James Farm Ecological Preserve on Cedar Neck Road in Ocean View, four miles west of Bethany Beach. This oasis of wild spaces on Indian River Bay is open to the public free of charge everyday from sunrise to sundown. There are three miles of marked hiking trails through seven different habitats carved out of this former 150-acre farm, from low marsh salty flats to the bayberry high marsh to a hardwood canopy of red oak, hickory, sweet gum, and sassafras. Guided kayak tours, offering eco tours and full moon excursions (as well as specially scheduled birthday parties) depart from James Farm. ∎

39375 Inlet Rd,
Rehoboth Beach, DE 19971
(302) 226-8105

CONVERSATION: CHRIS BASON

Executive Director, Delaware Center for the Inland Bays

THE INLAND BAYS

As an undergraduate at the University of Delaware, Chris Bason studied applied ecology and entomology ("UD has an amazing agricultural school, I was studying how to control bugs"). That led him to graduate school in wetland ecology. He started with the Delaware Center for the Inland Bays in 2004 as a research assistant and became director in 2012.

"Rehoboth Bay is a tidal water body that lies behind a barrier island that protects the bay from the sea. It's a very shallow coastal lagoon, three miles across at its widest.

In 'nature,' inlets on the coast are cut by storms and then periodically shoal over and reopen in different locations. That makes for a dynamic system of flushing in the estuary This changed in 1939 when the Army Corps of Engineers stabilized the Indian River Inlet, which connects the estuary to the Atlantic. This was done to support navigation and the commercial seafood industry of the Bays.

Everything was okay until the 1970s, when erosion below the surface started scouring the inlet. This allowed more and more water to flow into and out of the Bays. By the 1990s, the amount of water passing through the Indian River Inlet over one tide cycle had increased more than four times from what it had been in 1939. The result of this has been to turn the bays into something that is much more like ocean water than it once was.

This had a number of effects. It increased the tidal range of the bays. That extra foot of tide effects homeowners and makes big changes in the wetlands. With a lower tide, you have more difficulty navigating these naturally shallow waters. People think the bays have been silting in over time and that is true in many areas, but we are also experiencing much lower low tides due to the expansion of the inlet.

Nutrient pollution is the major problem facing the bay ecosystem, largely due to the leaching and run-off from agricultural and urban fertilizers, and atmospheric sources. Sussex County has one of the highest poultry densities in the country; in the past that led to a grand excess of chicken manure applied to fields as fertilizer and as a method of disposal. Our waters are particularly sensitive because the watershed is large, almost 300 square miles; it extends as far west as Georgetown, and the soils are sandy. Applying fertilizer in much of this area is like putting it into a big sandbox. Fifty percent of the fresh water entering the estuary is ground water seeping up from the aquifer. This groundwater carries with it to the bays the nutrients applied to the land that are not taken up in crops or vegetation.

Algae goes bonkers when you add all these nutrients. Waters that were once clear become murky and depleted of oxygen. Our bays are particularly polluted and this has had a negative impact on the underwater bay grasses which make an excellent habitat for fish. Sunlight is blocked at the surface by algae, it can't reach the bottom thus killing the grasses.

The fish community has correspondingly become less diverse. Seaweed, a kind of algae, had become so abundant that it smothered shellfish and fouled shorelines. At its height in 1956, nearly 18 million clams were harvested commercially in the inland bays. Today, the commercial harvest is around 1 million. Wild oysters, once scattered throughout the bay, have largely disappeared.

The good news is that we started seeing positive indicators of change with the 2011 State of the Bay report. There are big improvements in nutrient management thanks to reductions in manure and fertilizer applications, although this has not yet significantly reduced nutrient concentrations in the estuary itself. Point sources of nutrients from wastewater have been reduced by 85%. Nuisance abundances of seaweed have greatly declined. Some indicators of improved water quality are being observed that should allow for successful bay grass restoration. The changes we are seeing are the result of a great deal of cooperation and sacrifice from a community that works together. ∎

OYSTERS

Throughout much of its history, Rehoboth's claim to fame has been its oysters. It was a celebrated gastronomic delicacy for both Native Americans and early settlers. With the new millennium, however, the Rehoboth oyster has largely disappeared from the scene.

Now, though, there's good news. The taste of succulent, quality home-grown oysters may well be returning with the passage of an aquaculture bill designed to re-introduce oyster farming on leased tracts in the scenic inland bays.

Living in brackish habitats, oysters were once the dominant economic force here. Native American dumpsites were piled as high as a dozen feet with oyster shells on the banks of inlets like Rehoboth. During the early 1800s, harvesting oysters was so profitable that local newspapers referred to them as "White Gold."

However, by the middle of the 19th century the local oyster industry was in a bumpy retreat due to overharvesting and the shift in consumer palates for native clams. The oyster industry suffered further declines in the 1950s with the advent of the MSX disease and again in the 1990s with the infectious Dermo parasite, all of which finally put a stop to harvesting oysters in Delaware.

This was the state of the industry until disease resistant oysters began being introduced in neighboring states (they now generate over $100 million in revenues).

Oysters are filter feeders, drawing in water over their gills where they trap suspended plankton and other particles. As such, they contribute important environmental benefits. A single mature oyster can filter up to 50 gallons a day, removing fertilizer, sediments, and other organic waste. In one acre supporting maximum capacity oysters (750 thousand), upwards of 15 million gallons are filtered daily. For the relatively shallow waters of the inland bays, this means rapidly improved water quality. ■

By Robert Sturgeon

EATING OYSTERS IN THE LOCAL STYLE

Oyster harvesting still has a long way to go in Delaware and the Delaware Bay, meaning the raw bars here are serving oysters harvested elsewhere (mostly from Maine to Massachusetts, and North Carolina to Louisiana). Even so, one can still prepare 'foreign' oysters like a native :

Southern Delaware Fried Oysters

Approx. 24 oz. freshly shucked oysters, drained and patted dry. Check for shell pieces!
2.5 C saltine cracker crumbs and .5 C yellow corn meal, mixed thoroughly
2 eggs, beaten
3 Tbsp. cold water

Vegetable oil, enough for frying, heated to 365 degrees

Beat the water in with the eggs. Dip the dry oysters into the mixture, then dredge in the cracker/corn meal mixture, covering completely. Gently drop into the hot oil and fry about 2.5 minutes, turning gently until golden brown. Drain on a rack and serve Southern-style with cocktail sauce and a dollop of chicken salad. Yield: 6 servings.

Rehoboth Avenue Scalloped Oysters

Approx. 24 oz. freshly shucked oysters, drained (reserve the juice) and patted dry. Check for shell pieces!

2 C Panko breadcrumbs, lightly salted
½ C butter
2 eggs, beaten
1 tsp. salt
1 C half-and-half
¼ tsp. Tabasco pepper sauce (red)
1 tsp. Worcestershire sauce
Fresh parsley, finely chopped
Salt & Pepper

Put ½ C of the Panko into a lightly oiled 8" square baking dish. Place a layer of oysters (sprinkled with salt & pepper) in the bottom, followed by ½ of the butter and ½ of the remaining Panko. Continue layering in the same order to the top, starting with the remaining oysters, butter, and finishing with the Panko.

Combine the eggs, half-and-half, Tabasco, Worcestershire sauce and 1/3 C of the reserved oyster juice. Gently pour over the layered ingredients. Sprinkle with the chopped parsley. Bake at 350 degrees for about 40 minutes, or until lightly browned. Yield: 6 servings.

The Rehoboth Foodie
RehobothFoodie.com

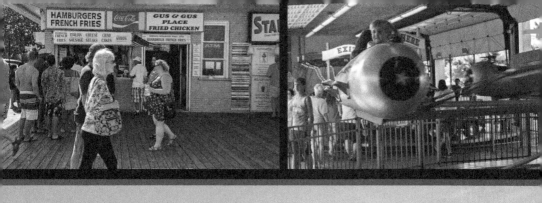

REHOBOTH
Boardwalk

DOLLE'S CANDYLAND

Dolle's Candyland stands at the foot of Rehoboth Avenue, a universally recognized icon that has anchored the boardwalk (some might say Rehoboth Beach, itself) for nearly a century.

Rudolph Dolle, a carousel maker, first came to the shore from his native New York to open an amusement attraction in Ocean City. A few years later, in 1910, he bought an adjoining salt-water taffy shop. In 1927, the present Rehoboth Beach location was opened, although that original building was destroyed in the nor'easter of 1962 and was built anew (the two-ton taffy machine washed onto the sand but was re-claimed and continues to stretch and wrap some 600 pieces per minute).

Now in its fourth generation of family operation, the business is run by Thomas Ibach, whose grandfather (originally a candy maker in Philadelphia) bought out Rudolph Dolle's interest in the business in 1959 but kept the its celebrated name.

What's Dolle's secret? A great location, to be sure. But beyond that, they differ from most beach-front confectioners because they continue to make their own chocolates, toffee (peanut butter is the favorite flavor), and fabled caramel corn. ∎

WHAT IS SALT WATER TAFFY?

Salt-water taffy is false advertising (but who cares)! Its main ingredients are corn syrup, glycerin, butter and flavoring that are boiled into a sticky mass and then aerated to become light, fluffy and chewy. Nothing at all to do with salt water!

Why, then, the name? Taffy pulls, it turns out, were popular entertainment with Atlantic City vacationers in the late 19th century. People wanted to bring taffy home as a souvenir from the beach.

A bad storm in 1883 soaked a storekeeper's entire stock with ocean water. So legend goes, a young girl later entered his shop asking for taffy and he offered her the only thing he had, "salt water taffy." She was thrilled at this exotic 'new' concoction. So were others. A legendary product was born. A trademark registered for the name "salt water taffy" was granted and then subsequently invalidated as the name was, by then, in common use.

WCTU FOUNTAIN
'DRINK WATER, NOT WHISKEY'

At their national organizing convention in 1874, the Woman's Christian Temperance Union urged its anti-alcohol members to erect sanitary public drinking fountains around the country so men could 're-fresh' themselves without having to enter a saloon for stronger stuff. Not such a crazy idea, since water was less safe than beer at the time.

Sussex County had already been dry for over a decade when Prohibition passed in 1919. Not everybody was happy. Bootleggers operated off the Rehoboth Bay, Whiskey Beach near Gordon's Pond got its name as a convenient drop-off site.

The Rehoboth fountain, honed out of a six-foot chunk of granite, was erected in 1929 to commemorate the 50th anniversary of the founding of the Delaware branch of the WCTU.

"It has been here operating through hurricanes, nor'easters and the famous storm of '62," said Evelyn D. Thoroughgood at the ceremony marking its inclusion to the National Register of Historic Places in 2009. "This is where parents dropped their kids off, dates met each other. This was the big meeting place in the center of Rehoboth." ∎

"WALKING THE BOARDS"

By Rich Barnett

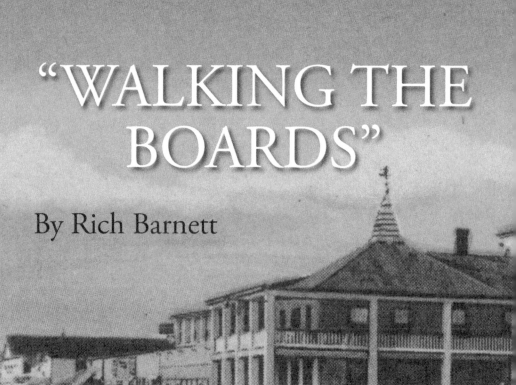

Rehobothians have a love-hate relationship with their Boardwalk, named by The Travel Channel and *National Geographic* as one of the country's best. Some say it's overcrowded and tacky and smells of suntan lotion and French fries. It does. Others recognize it as an enduring symbol of the classic family beach vacation. It is. Whatever your feelings, to know Rehoboth you gotta "walk the boards."

ATLANTIC CITY: THE ORIGINAL BOARDWALK

During the early 1800s, the few towns found at the Jersey Shore remained small fishing hamlets with perhaps hunting lodges in the marshes. By the late century, though, as railroads made shore towns accessible to visitors from New York and Philadelphia, more and more people began to come.

Hotel owners and railroad conductors became concerned about beach sand being tracked onto lobby carpets and into railroad cars. A conductor on the Atlantic City-Camden Railroad was asked to solve the problem. His solution: eight-foot planks of wood arranged in a herringbone pattern atop a substructure of concrete and steel to serve as a walkway. These first boardwalks were temporary structures, removed and stored the end of the season.

The first boardwalks were built in Cape May in 1868. Two years later, Atlantic City followed with a raised boardwalk.

Boardwalks evolved from a practical way of getting to and from the beach and a kind of 'fashion walkway for the wealthy' to a commercial enterprise carrying tourists from hotels to hawkers. Amusement piers were added by the turn-of-the-20th century.

The mile-long Boardwalk as we know it today was built in 1905. Shorter versions date back to 1873. The earliest editions were simply planks of wood laid on the sand. The Rehoboth Boardwalk has been damaged by big storms in 1914, 1962, 1992, and 1998, and rebuilt each time – thankfully of wood, not concrete and plastic as in other towns. Can a boardwalk truly be called a boardwalk if it isn't made of wooden boards?

The perfect starting point to "walk the boards" is at the north end in front of the imposing white-block Henlopen Hotel. The Henlopen is one of Rehoboth's oldest hotels, built back in 1879, to replace the Surf Hotel, which burned down. The original Henlopen was five stories and constructed of Sussex County timber. One of Rehoboth's finest, it featured high ceilings and wraparound porches designed to catch the Atlantic breezes back in the days before air conditioning. Rooms at the turn of the century rented for $10 per week. It was a swinging hot spot for big bands and dancing in the 1940s and 1950s. Naturally, the hotel has changed quite a bit over the years. It's currently both a hotel and a private condominium. The view of the coastline and the town from the top of the building is pretty amazing.

Keeping Rehoboth an attractive resort destination isn't easy

Boardwalk South from Horn's, Rehoboth Beach, Del.

and it isn't cheap. Take beach replenishment. Every three years or so, 1.7 million cubic yards of sand are pumped from offshore to renourish Rehoboth's beach and dune system at a cost of about $4 million.

A nice sandy beach is the engine that drives Rehoboth's tourist economy. The sand dunes provide protection against damaging coastal storms by absorbing wave energy. Dune Nature Park showcases all sorts of native plants that thrive in the dunes: goldenrod, yucca, sweet peas, prickly pear cactus, scrub pines, and, of course, beach grasses.

To help stabilize the sand, volunteers each spring plant stems of beach grass all along the dunes on the east side of the Boardwalk. Cape American beach grass is the varietal of choice. Its roots can go down eighteen inches. Its blades help trap wind blown sand, which can create new dunes and expand existing dunes.

Beach grass is amazingly tolerant of high salinity conditions, direct sun, extreme heat, lack of fertile soil, and a fluctuating water supply. The plant has developed a thick brittle stalk, which unfortunately snaps easily when trampled by vehicle or feet. That's why you see the "keep off the dune" signs. The graceful serpentine wooden dune fences also trap sand.

Most people probably assume the white house with the big front porch beside the Dune Nature Park is a private home. And it is. Sort of. The Pennsylvania Railroad built it in 1921 for its employees use. Now it's run and maintained by a private association of retired and former railroad employees.

Founded in 1846, the Pennsylvania Railroad grew to become the largest publicly traded corporation in the world, with a budget larger than that of the U.S. government and a workforce of about a quar-

On the Boardwalk, Rehoboth Beach, Del.

ter of a million people. It owned most lines that served Delaware. The railroad came to Rehoboth in 1878 and was instrumental in helping turn the town from a quiet religious resort into a secular resort open to the general public. The first road into Rehoboth wasn't completed until 1925.

Next landmark along the way is the small monument to Giovanni da Verrzanao, the Italian explorer who was the earliest European 'officially' to explore the coast. It was erected in 2008 and sits upon stone from Verrazano's ancestral hometown in Italy. In case you're wondering,

this is the same Verrazano who discovered New York harbor (the bridge connecting Staten Island and Brooklyn was named in his honor) and was later killed and eaten by natives during a Caribbean expedition in 1528.

Stop and pose at the "your face here" Victorian family cut-out in front of the Boardwalk Plaza Hotel. Getting dressed up and strolling the Boardwalk was a popular summer pastime in Rehoboth up until World War II.

Rehoboth's lifeguards don't stroll; they patrol, and have done so since 1921. Drop by the Beach Patrol headquarters on

the boardwalk at Baltimore Avenue and check out the guard activity. During peak summer in July, beach patrols from Delaware and Maryland compete in a variety of running, swimming, and tugging events during the annual Lifeguard Olympics on the beach in front of headquarters. Another tradition is the lifeguard photo where they pose in their signature red suits for a squad photo that then becomes a postcard. They've been doing it for decades.

Dolle's is another Boardwalk tradition, best known for its looming orange sign and salt water taffy. Dolle's opened in 1927. Salt water taffy is thequintessential souvenir of a trip to the seashore and synonymous with boardwalks all along the Atlantic shore. Confectioners make the taffy on premises at Dolle's. The caramel corn is pretty good too.

How about a cool drink of water? One of the few remaining temperance fountains in America can be found on the Boardwalk

at the foot of Rehoboth Avenue. It seems a tad quaint today, but temperance (aka Prohibition) was a divisive political and social issue in this country. The six-foot tall, three-foot wide, granite water fountain was erected in 1929 by the Women's Christian Temperance Union (WCTU) to commemorate the 50th anniversary of the Delaware branch of the organization and to encourage people to quench their thirst with water, not booze.

Temperance wasn't the only attempt Rehoboth made to control "morality."

Men used to be fined for walking shirtless on the boardwalk. Certainly, there were some fellas who ought to have kept a shirt on. But to legislate it?

In 1937, Rehoboth Beach passed Ordinance 18 calling for a $5 fine for unduly and improper exposure of his or her person on any beach or strand, boardwalk, or other public place within the City. It went on to say that male bathers could remove their top on the beach "east" of the Boardwalk and weren't subject to this provision. The city affirmed the ban in 1975, triggered supposedly because a city employee was spotted working outside without his shirt on.

It wasn't until July 1980 that it finally became legal for men to walk on the Boardwalk without a shirt. That year, the City, in a 5-2 vote repealed its ordinance requiring males over the age of 5 to wear shirts on the Boardwalk after 6 p.m. and to wear shirts at all times "west of the Boardwalk."

Luckily, Rehoboth hasn't tried to legislate eating. Pizza, for example, is a boardwalk favorite and popular history says this tradition began on Coney Island in the 1920s. Grotto Pizza is Rehoboth's original pizza parlor, founded in 1960. For more

than a half century, Thrasher's has been serving up hot tubs of French fries. Rehoboth style means a lot of salt and a few shakes of vinegar. The seagulls are fond of them too, and it's always entertaining when a hungry gull snatches a fry right out of the greasy fingers of some unsuspecting child.

Fans of 50s retro should check out Gus and Gus, a family-run grill on the Boardwalk at Wilmington Avenue. Founded in 1956, the establishment serves up hamburgers, hot dogs, fried chicken, French fries, and cheesesteaks. Eat in or order to go. If only the table top jukeboxes still worked.

Just south of Wilmington Avenue is Ryan's, an arcade and t-shirt shop that's been around since 1961. There's mini golf on the roof. It's a no-frills course and a nod to the game's humble origins. But

THE ASH WEDNESDAY STORM OF 1962

Before the Storm, circa. 1960

After the Storm

Photo credit: Alan Broadbent & Faye Nadia Parsons

The Ash Wednesday Storm of 1962 remains the *storm of record* in Delaware for tide heights, its nine feet topping even Hurricane Sandy in 2013. For a three-day period stretching through five high tides it stalled over the east coast, pounding coastal areas with continuous rain, high winds, and tidal surges.

Sand dunes were flattened along the entire length of the Delaware coastline.

Along Rehoboth Beach, erosion was devastating. Beachfront hotels were destroyed, structures washed into the sea, and the boardwalk reduced to splinters. Bumper cars from Playland were discovered at either end of the boardwalk.

what do you want for $4 and a great view of the ocean? The arcade also has one of those old school photo booths where you go behind the curtain, slip in some coins, and come out with a strip of photos.

Four generations of the Fasnacht family have operated Funland amusement park. On summer nights, it's jammed with screaming children, love-struck teens, and the occasional hot daddy. Tickets for rides only cost 35 cents. Grab a seat in front of the swinging Viking ship and you'll sail within 5 feet of the neighbor's living room window and get an interesting behind the scenes look at the Boardwalk. The old fashioned Funland experience was the subject of a 2004 film by Delawarean Sharon Kelly Baker entitled "Nothing Beats Fun: The Funland Story."

Storms have left their imprint on the Boardwalk. On April 14, 1918, extreme easterly winds forced the 640 ton *Merrimac* onto Rehoboth Beach. The *Merrimac* came to rest at the foot of Brooklyn Avenue in front of the St. Agnes by the Sea convent (which was torn down and replaced by the Star of the Sea Motel which was torn down and replaced by the current Star of the Sea condominium building). The *Merrimac* sunk so deep into the sand that it couldn't be pulled off the beach. So the town just stripped off the top and left it.

On September 14, 1944, hurricane-force winds drove the 2443 ton *S.S. Thomas Tracy* onto the beach and right on top of the *Merrimac*. Seriously. The Coast Guard couldn't remove it, so they dismantled it down to the waterline and just left it there. The town has cordoned off the area to protect swimmers. Before the beach replenishment you could see the remains of the shipwrecks.

The Star of the Sea is also symbolic of the battle in Rehoboth over building heights. After the condo was built, the city put a height limit on buildings to prevent the beach from being shaded by tall buildings like what happened down the road in Ocean City, Maryland.

The southern Boardwalk is quieter and more residential. That is until you come to the end and notice all the Vespas, bicycles, and throngs of men in stylish bathing suits. Yep, you've arrived at Poodle Beach, a gay magnet since the 1970s and recognized today as one of America's favorite gay beaches.

Gay guys have been hanging out on this part of the beach since the 70s when it was called Carpenter's Beach. Back in the 30s and 40s, du Pont heiress and well-known lesbian Louisa (du Pont) Carpenter entertained her gay and lesbian and bisexual theatre and Hollywood friends on the beach in front of the family compound, which still stands. It's the handsome shingled house with the big fireplaces just above where they sell hot dogs and Italian ices on the beach.

Speaking of coifs, Labor Day features drag volleyball on Poodle Beach. What began as a pick-up game twenty years ago has evolved into a bona fide tradition of costumes, camp, political satire, and coordinated dance routines. Men in swimsuits ring the volleyball court, disco music is blasting, and the overflow crowd stretches along the Boardwalk from Prospect Street to Queen Street. It's quite a scene.

At this point, you need to walk over to the fence at the end of the Boardwalk and give it a good slap. You've officially "walked the boards" and, hopefully, learned a little about Rehoboth. Now turn around and walk it again. This time you can stop for a tub of fries. ■

FUNLAND

From May to September each year, the heart of Rehoboth Beach arguably moves to Funland, the seaside stretch between Delaware and Brooklyn Avenues. This enduring, family-run boardwalk amusement park with permanent, stationary rides has been holding down oceanfront enjoyment for all ages since 1962.

In 1961, Al and Sis Fasnacht visited Rehoboth Beach with their two sons and daughters-in-law for some R&R on the Atlantic. The Fasnacht family owned and operated what they refer to as a small 'picnic park' in Harrisburg, Pennsylvania.

At that time, there was a boardwalk amusement park called the Rehoboth Beach Sports Center and Playland, owned by the Dentino family. The two families struck up a conversation, the Dentinos wanted out of the park business, and offered to sell. Although tempted, the Fasnachts decided it was a pipedream and returned home to Hershey.

Whatever the reason—a cold Pennsylvania winter or a new affection for Rehoboth—by the following spring the Fasnachts changed their minds and decided to go for it. The settlement was arranged for March 15, 1962.

As the talks were concluding, an area of low pressure was developing off the Atlantic. On March 6, an almost-hurricane fueled by the convergence of three low-pressure systems and a tide-rising alignment of the sun and moon created what is now known as the Great Storm of '62, the worst Nor'easter of the 20th century (only Hurricane Sandy has ever done more damage). It devastated Rehoboth, ripping up the boardwalk and causing massive destruction to Playland.

After the storm, the two families reconnoitered. Despite the wallop this storm delivered, they decided to proceed with the deal. Against all odds, the boardwalk was re-built and Funland opened for business that summer.

Since then, four generations of the Fasnacht family have returned to Rehoboth each summer to run their amusement park, employing thousands of park attendants —typically high school or college students on vacation.

The thing that makes Funland so special are its rides and games, old-time in spirit and often in fact. Many have been around for generations, offering time-travel into an earlier era of state fairs and carnivals.

Boats

These two-seater skiffs have ferried the youngest generations since 1952, pre-dating Funland itself, eight boats circling around the watchful eye of a mermaid.

Bumper Cars

This action-packed ride also pre-dates Funland, but has undergone renovations through the years. The bumper cars these days are actually powered through the floor, but a glance above reveals the grid and other remnants of the older, ceiling-powered cars.

Derby

The Derby game attracts attention from its pole position right on the boards. A skee-ball style horse race pits as many as ten players against one another excitedly aiming for the blue holes to advance their horse fastest across the finish line.

Haunted Mansion

A later addition, the Haunted Mansion has become somewhat of a rite-of-passage for kids who grew up visiting Rehoboth. This is the only ride at the park that doesn't open until nighttime to increase the fear-factor. The recent addition of a rollercoaster-style photo booth captures the frightened faces of riders busy being spooked.

Merry-Go-Round

The carousel survived the storm of '62, but has undergone some minor cosmetic touch-ups through the years. With 30 original horses and two chariots, this ride is friendly to parents, children and even the horse-averse.

Paratrooper

The Paratrooper joined the Funland lineup in 1981, bringing a Ferris-wheel ride into the mix and providing riders a birds-eye view of the beach. Ten parachute-style cars that can hold up to four people apiece comprise this high-flying classic. Although it may seem relatively tame, when the Paratrooper switches into reverse riders experience a momentary dose of stomach dropping.

ROADWAY Tours

R oadway tours by bike or car (or, for the fit, even by foot) take travellers 2.5 miles north or south from the heart of town at Rehoboth Avenue and the boards – the Woman's Christian Temperance Union Fountain

The northbound 'Sunrise' tour starts up Rehoboth Avenue for a couple of blocks and then, at the second stop light, turns right on (you guessed it) 2nd Street. The trail winds through residences, past ocean views and the up-scale communities of North Shores and Henlopen Acres (it's own independent high-dollar municipality). The end destination is one of the most treasured local inside spots, Gordon's Pond at Cape Henlopen State Park and the brand new, million-dollar off-road bike trail (where a whole new set of adventures awaits).

The southbound 'Sunset' trail heads up Rehoboth Avenue as well but this time make a left on 1st Street (when left turns at stoplights are no longer permissible in-season, make a U-turn just past the stoplight, and turn right on 1st Street from the east-bound side of Rehoboth Avenue). This trip runs south around beautiful Silver Lake and then into Dewey Beach.

A note of caution. Traffic along the main drags can be intense in-season. Please be advised to obey moving vehicle laws and wear a helmet for safety. Although a ride on the boardwalk is always tempting, bicycles are only permitted on the boardwalk from sunrise to 10 a.m. from May to September (restrictions loosen in the off-season).

One more thing. Police give tickets in-season for reckless bicycling!

By Molly MacMillan

courtesy of Portraits in the Sand

NORTH SHORE SUNRISE BICYCLE TOUR

ROUTE

- REHOBOTH AVENUE WEST (RIGHT) TO 2ND STREET
- 2ND ST (RIGHT) TO OLIVE AVE
- OLIVE AVE (LEFT) TO 1ST ST
- 1ST ST (RIGHT) TO LAKE AVE
- LAKE AVE TO END OF BOARDS (LEFT) BECOMES SURF AVE
- SURF AVE TO STOP SIGN (RIGHT) ON OCEAN DRIVE
- OCEAN DRIVE TO CAPE HENLOPEN STATE PARK
- END AT PAVILLION GORDON'S POND

A wonderful way to start the day is with a ride along the boardwalk—that is, until 10 a.m., after which bikes are barred from the boards. For those eager for a north-bound tour of town, it's easy to veer off to chase the sunrise eastward along Surf Avenue.

This road-route through the north side of town offers the idyllic essence of Rehoboth Beach as a peaceful retreat and refuge. From the simple cottages and less simple oceanfront mansions, the mood through the leafy streets is as old-timey as drinking hand-squeezed lemonade in a rocker on the front porch.

From the Temperance Fountain on Rehoboth Avenue, go two blocks

west and turn right on 2nd Street at the FDR-funded Depression-era post office. Inside, the post office proudly displays a piece of New Deal oil-on-canvas artwork called "Frontier Mail" painted by Karl Knaths and commissioned in 1940 by a federal program to support the arts (and starving artists).

Turning right on 2nd Street, one

comes to the calming vista of Lake Gerar just past Oliver Avenue. One of three freshwater ponds in Rehoboth, Lake Gerar was mostly swampland until Irenee DuPont (President of DuPont from 1919-1926)struck up a deal with the city. In return for draining the swamp, creating a proper park, and helping to stabilize some cash-starved local banks, he received rights to ten acres of land surrounding the lake. He sub-divided it into lots to form the "Rehoboth Cottage Club", intended to be a collection of congenial people and 'modest' rather than self-consciously grand houses. DuPont pressured residents not to cut down trees and preserve dirt roads for the rustic effect (one block of Pine Avenue remains unpaved to this day).

Bear right on Olive Avenue and

make a left turn on 1st Street to continue over the bridge at Lake Gerar. Turn right on the Lake Avenue extension and prepare for a new view on the approach to a picturesque scene of beach grass, dunes and the expansive Atlantic.

Bear left on Surf Avenue to continue past beach entry paths for sunbathers and a pine tree border shielding beach dunes and tennis courts before reaching the stop at Surf Avenue and Ocean Drive.

You have two choices on how to proceed:

Straight ahead at this juncture leads into Henlopen Acres, a high-end enclave of architecturally historic homes nestled in a leafy, forested setting. A 69-household municipality of its own, Henlopen Acres is the smallest and only purely residential town in the state, as well as having the second-highest per-capita income.

Turning right on Ocean Drive brings cyclists past the public tennis courts at Deauville Beach and to the left, the community of North Shores. Though cyclists will be flanked on either side by private tennis courts for the communities of North Shores and Henlopen Acres, only the tennis courts at Deauville Beach are open to the public.

Ride past gentle dunes and grasses lining the sandy coast, a pastoral interlude of extraordinary peace compared to more populated beach-fronts further south. This stretch gives visitors a glimpse of Rehoboth Beach at its best.

Ocean Drive leads directly in to the Gordon's Pond segment of Cape

Henlopen State Park where a shaded pavilion with a dozen picnic tables provides a place to dismount and gaze in rapture at the Atlantic Ocean just over the dunes.

But for those who are just starting to get warmed up, another, off-road op-

tion also exists here at Gordon's Pond. Near the pavilion, an off-road trailhead picks up, taking riders around Gordon's Pond on packed soil and boardwalk trailway through Cape Henlopen State Park and into Lewes.

LAKE GERAR

59 Lake Avenue is still a legendary address to some old-time Rehoboth townies that can recall Bob Ching's White Chimney Inn located there, the scene of one of Rehoboth's most heinous crimes. Ching could often be seen fishing on the shores of Lake Gerar to catch snapping turtles he used for special soups (fishing is permitted in certain areas of the pond with a valid fishing license). On the eve of Thanksgiving in 1969, the town awoke to find that Ching had been murdered by his long-time cook, who then took his own life.

'FRONTIER MAIL'

Karl Knaths, born in Wisconsin in 1891, was an early modernist who worked in a cubist idiom deeply influenced by Cezanne. He lived most of his life amongst the colony of artists and writers in Provincetown, Massachusetts. Noted for murals, his work is in the collection of the Metropolitan Museum and the Whitney Museum in New York, the Museum of Fine Arts in Boston, and the Art Institute of Chicago.

"Frontier Mail" is one of seven post office murals in Delaware from the New Deal era. Three feet tall and ten feet long, it depicts an African-American mailman striding away from a trading post toward his Appaloosa horse, watched by a shopkeeper as a barefooted mother and daughter enter the store to buy groceries.

GORDONS POND

BY DENNIS FORNEY
PUBLISHER, CAPE GAZETTE

A few centuries back, when round, blue-and-yellow containers of salt weren't so plentiful on our grocery-store shelves, European settlers in these parts looked to the sea for this valuable spice. It's believed that Gordons Pond started out as a man-made impoundment for the gathering of sea salt.

Men cut channels across the beach and through the dunes to allow high ocean tides to fill sand-bottomed flats contained within hand-shoveled dikes. After the sun evaporated much of the water, the remaining super-salty liquid would then be bucketed into large cast-iron pots and boiled off over driftwood or pine-bough fires. The process provided a steady supply of salt to preserve meat and fish for the settlers.

One of those historic pots sits in front of Rehoboth Art League's Homestead Mansion in Henlopen Acres, the 17th century home of generations of the Marsh family who mined their salt in this fashion.

That helps explain why the hard sand bottom of Gordons Pond is actually above the normal high tides in the surrounding salt marsh. These days, it's only a rare and powerful nor'easter that breaks through the dunes every 10 years or so to push ocean water into Gordons Pond.

Since controlling mosquito populations is a major consideration in a shallow salt-marsh pond like Gordons, Delaware's Mosquito Control manages the gates that control water levels there. Two gates – one at the northwest corner of the pond and another at the southwest corner – serve to either drain water or allow water in from high tides flooding Lewes-Rehoboth Canal. Water-levels are also managed for waterfowl, shorebirds, fish, crustaceans and shoreline vegetation.

The original Gordons Pond, deep enough for boaters to use for fishing and sailing, was located approximately where the Henlopen Acres Marina is now situated. Fed By Rehoboth Creek, the pond apparently was a casualty of the construction, in the early 1900s, of Lewes-Rehoboth Canal to connect Lewes Creek to the north and Rehoboth Creek to the south as a commercially navigable connection between Delaware Bay and Rehoboth Bay.

Although the original pond went away, the name – like waterfowl in the spring – survived by migrating to the north. Or, maybe, it's all that salt that led to the name's preservation. ■

THE GLORY OF
GORDONS POND

ROUTE

- REHOBOTH WEST TO TURNABOUT ON LEFT, 2ND BLOCK AT ATLANTIS INN
- REHOBOTH AVE TO 1ST ST (NOW ON RIGHT AFTER TURNABOUT)
- 1ST ST BECOMES KING CHARLES (@ WESTMINSTER PRESBYTERIAN)

SUNDOWN TO DEWEY

- FOLLOW TO SILVER LAKE (RIGHT) ON LAKE DRIVE
- LAKE DRIVE (LEFT) TO SILVER LAKE DRIVE
- AFTER LAKE COMEGYS, LEFT @ STOPLIGHT TO SOUTHBOUND ROUTE 1
- PASS STARBOARD, BOTTLE AND CORK, RT ON DICKINSON ST END @ RUSTY RUDDER, DICKINSON ST/BAY

Here's a tranquil ride for the shank of the day, when you're feeling mellow and primed to savor a beautiful sunset over Rehoboth Bay.

Road-riding south of Rehoboth Avenue offers another 2.5-mile trek filled with new vistas of beach life that take riders through the heart of Rehoboth's younger sister city of Dewey Beach.

Beginning at the fountain on Rehoboth Avenue, proceed due west on the avenue for the southern tour. This trip requires a left-hand turn onto First Street and because this is prohibited in-season, continue straight under the first green light and make the next legal U-turn, then right on First Street (a word of warning, seasonal police officers will ticket bicyclists for traffic violations without hesitation!).

After this little maneuver, First Street will take riders away from some of the congestion of Rehoboth Avenue. Several blocks after the avenue, First Street becomes King Charles Avenue and widens, with Westminster Presbyterian and St. Edmunds Catholic Church facing due east.

Cycling past beach blocks from Laurel to St. Lawrence Streets, King Charles Avenue leads directly to Silver Lake, a 45-acre freshwater lake and waterfowl refuge that is home to returning flocks of canvasback ducks and Canada geese. Stay to the right on Lake Drive and pass beach cottages and spectacular white gazebos that are privately owned and constructed by the homeowners.

In the late 1980s and 1990s, Lake Drive was also home to a more exotic bird-watching experience when a flock of hardy Monk Parakeets took up residence in the utility poles along this roadway. Believed to be the offspring of escapees from a shipwrecked cargo vessel, the birds built massive nests in the telephone poles and kept watch over the lake for nearly 20 years. Unfortunately, these nests grew to such epic proportions weighing down utility lines that they had to be removed, but local birders report cold-tolerant, long-lived Monk Parakeets continue to be spotted elsewhere in the region.

At the stop sign on Lake Drive, turn left on Bayard Avenue, which becomes Sil-

• •

MONK PARAKEETS SET UP RESIDENCE

About 200 of the pretty South American birds have taken up residence in Rehoboth Beach, where to some local residents they are unwelcome destroyers of fruit crops.

The hardy birds are native to Argentina and Bolivia. But they began showing up in Rehoboth in the late 1980s.

"When a flock goes by, it sounds like the Exotic Bird section of a pet shop," said one local observer. "What a racket!! The parrots roost in the banks of outdoor lights and around power transformers. The community-nests that they construct - mainly from twigs and branches - are very large, holding dozens of birds. It's an incredible sight to see!"

The Reading Eagle, 1996

ST. EDMOND CATHOLIC CHURCH

In 1905, the Catholic Diocese of Wilmington purchased property, running the full length of the oceanfront block between Laurel Street and Brooklyn Avenue for the construction of St. Agnes. It consisted of a rectory and a chapel along with two large cottages for the Franciscan teaching and nursing order as a summer vacation retreat for the nuns.

The increasing number of Catholics in the area, along with the exposure to storm damage because of the ocean front location, prompted the creation of a new church at the present location in 1940. It was named in honor of St. Edmond, Archbishop of Canterbury in the 13th century who incurred the enmity of King Henry III and was forced to flee to France.

WESTMINSTER PRESBYTERIAN CHURCH

Westminster Presbyterian Church has sat at the corner of King Charles and Laurel Streets in Rehoboth Beach, Delaware, since the early 1930's, when the Midway Presbyterian Church (Route 1) decided a second Presbyterian presence was needed "in town," to provide worship and ministry for the tourists.

ver Lake Drive over the bridge, and continue south toward Dewey Beach. In contrast to Coastal Highway, the main beach throughway, this route is a safer, more scenic alternative to the traffic along the "forgotten mile" between Rehoboth and Dewey

As cyclists pass Silver Lake to the left, the cozy vista of Lake Comegys will emerge to the right. Early in the 1800s, Silver Lake and Lake Comegys were conjoined, at which time the Comegys extension was already known as Tan Vat Cove. Just after this second freshwater lake, the elaborate homes and condos with views of Silver Lake become seasoned beach cottages with screened-in porches and a pine-tree property lines.

Eventually this route leads to a stoplight on Coastal Highway at Dewey Beach city limits. Make a left turn at the stoplight to ride along southbound Coastal Highway – the one-and-only north-south main street – through the heart of Dewey Beach. Just after this turn, visitors are greeted by a sign that reads: "Dewey Beach, a Way of Life," and virtually anyone who has visited this seaside town can verify the truth of this statement.

The ride along Coastal Highway will bring cyclists past some of the landmarks of Dewey culture, starting with the Starboard Restaurant on Salisbury Street and Coastal Highway. In-season, the streets of Dewey Beach are packed with parked cars and vacationers en-route to the beach or the bar. As always, ride defensively and be aware of barriers along the roadway to curtail stumbling into traffic.

Next up, the Bottle and Cork, founded in 1936 on Bellevue Street and the highway, calls itself "The Greatest Rock-n-Roll Bar in the World," and for three months of the year, it may just be. Booking acts like Dave Matthews Band, Pete Yorn and Blondie over the summer and hosting a jam session every Saturday afternoon keeps Dewey Beach in tune with its rock-n-roll lifestyle.

Continuing a few more blocks south, the Rusty Rudder on Dickinson Street and the bay offers an opportunity to dismount and catch sunset on Rehoboth Bay. Every evening, the bar with a massive deck on the water hosts a calypso band, serves 20-ounce "Sunset Sipper" cocktails and light fare from an outside grill. On any given day, the dock will be brimming with boats, the volleyball court alive with sport and the bar a hub of sunset-sipping activity.

And just in case the island music and relaxed atmosphere turns one sunset sipper turns into two, Dickinson Street is also a central hub for public transport. Busses back to Rehoboth have bike racks and the Jolly Trolley accepts bicycles on a case-by-case basis. ■

SILVER LAKE

Silver Lake, given this name in 1924 to promote the adjoining real estate development of Rehoboth Heights, has long been prized along the Atlantic coast as a fresh water lake extremely close to the ocean.

The Nanticoke tribe, whose home base was on the north shore of Indian River Bay, regularly encamped at the lake to gather clams and oysters that were smoked to provide food well into winter. It was also used to trade with inland tribes, particularly for the hard stone Pennsylvania Jasper that could be finely honed into arrowheads.

In Colonial days, Silver Lake was a handy place for ship captains to secure fresh water before heading out to sea. This was especially true of pirates preparing for a marauding mission. Indeed, the settlers of Lewes sent armed men here several times to prevent pirates from filling their casks.

Before ice was commercially produced, farmers would cut blocks from Silver Lake and use them to prevent foodstuffs from spoiling.

Now a designated waterfowl preserve, Silver Lake's 45-acres provides habitat to a variety of ducks, geese and other types of freshwater birds throughout the year, making it a favored site for wildlife photographers.

The oceanfront property between Silver Lake and the ocean was originally owned by Irene Carpenter Draper, a member of the DuPont family, and then inherited by her five daughters. In the late 1990s, a subdivision was approved requiring half-acre lots (the two original Carpenter homes still exist). With spectacular views of both the Atlantic and Silver Lake, the homes here are prized (the last transaction was in 2003) and conservatively valued in excess of $6 million. ∎

DEWEY BEACH

Dewey Beach came into being in 1885 as a distinct entity when Clementine and Robert West bought 135 acres of land from John Roades, the strip extending from the north end of Lake Comegys and Silver Lake, all the way south to the bay. Known as Rehoboth City in the earliest days of settlement, Dewey Beach was renamed for Admiral George Dewey, who became a national hero after winning the 1898 Battle of Manila during the Spanish-American War.

About a mile long and two blocks wide, Dewey is a sliver of land separating Rehoboth Bay from the Atlantic. The population of 341 year-round residents can swell to more than 30,000 on summer weekends.

More than a dozen bars and restaurants are packed into this narrow strip of land with a long history as a seaside watering hole. During the era when Rehoboth was a 'dry' Methodist summer meeting camp, arid campers would travel a mile south to quench their thirst at a 'hotel' that served beer and whiskey on the outskirts of Dewey.

There's a lot of ways to have a good time here outside the bars. With its dynamic topography and beachside activities including bonfires and a beach movie night each week, Dewey is also building a reputation as a family-friendly resort.

Dewey Beach is known for its younger population, partial to daytime sports activities like volleyball, and supreme skim boarding. Rehoboth Bay offers safe harbor for small watercraft, paddleboards and jet skis. Bottom line: Dewey Beach offers the opportunity to see the sunrise—and sunset— on the water with plenty of ways to fill the time in-between. ∎

DEWEY BEACH, A COMING OF AGE TALE

By Molly MacMillan

My first job was at a small sub shop, JJ's Corner Market, across the street from the Starboard when I was 15. My girl friend's uncle owned the store. I helped out over 4th of July weekend and that evolved into a full time summer job.

I quickly caught on to a decidedly adult view of Dewey Beach from this vantage point. Other kids scoop ice cream for their first job at the beach; I sold cigarettes, coffee, and prophylactics to a week-end population of D.C. yuppies eager to cut loose.

From behind the sales counter we'd be grabbing pastries, snatching up Gatorades, and tossing breakfast sandwiches like hot potatoes. On a busy morning , when we were fielding cigarette and over-the-counter painkiller requests for the throngs of over-hung weekend warriors, the line flowed out the door.

The air conditioner was always broken or rendered useless by the open doors, bakery oven and grill, so we made up reasons to visit the walk-in-freezer outdoors for relief.

When I wasn't working, I tagged along with my 21 year old sister. Her six friends had a beach cottage on Buena Street: two screened-in porches, three bedrooms, and one bathroom. This is the typical schematic in Dewey, unless the housemates decide to buy into a larger place with more beds and sell weekend shares——a practice that could add dozens to the household count..

I would subsequently spend more summers working at the beach, but the next job for me was in Rehoboth. By my senior summer, just before college, I was living in an apartment steps off the boardwalk. Hanging out underage in downtown Rehoboth, my friends and I would spend a lot of time with the kids who worked at Funland. They were mostly from England and Ireland and notorious for throwing wild parties (more than a few properties were devastated after a night of rowdy drinking).

At 19, it was back to Dewey Beach, this time as a waitress which I would do for a number of summers.

To say that beach life got lively would be an understatement. The restaurant and hospitality complexes in the area employed hundreds of my contemporaries so there was always a party.

Days were filled with beach volleyball, nights consumed with tournaments of beer-pong (or 'Beirut' as the boys from Baltimore called it). At least once a once a summer we would charter a 'booze cruise' and set sail down the Lewes-Rehoboth Canal or on a pontoon in the bay.

One summer, my childhood musical idol Cyndi Lauper came to play the Bottle & Cork (still the best venue to catch big acts). I was finally 21. My collegiate crew of co-workers and I went to see her and confirm what we already suspected: in Dewey Beach, girls did just want to have fun!

Dewey remains a party town today, but as my generation of Dewey Beach-goers has grown up, so has the town also evolved to offer more than a good drink. The bar scene is still an adventure, but now there are family activities like movie nights and bonfires on the beach, skim camps and parasailing.

Here's the best way I can describe how Dewey has changed over the years. Now, when you spot a stroller being pushed down the sidewalk along Coastal Highway, there is most likely a baby inside. But I remember, 'back in the days,' when the only baby carriages you saw in Dewey Beach were hauling kegs. ∎

JUNCTION AND BREAKWATER TRAIL REHOBOTH TO LEWES

Just when the hustle and bustle of downtown Rehoboth Beach in-season becomes overwhelming, rest easy; the Junction and Breakwater Trail from Rehoboth to Lewes offers an opportunity for an escapist to get lost in the countryside running, cycling or hiking.

Not only is this ride a more peaceful, healthy alternative to driving between Rehoboth and Lewes, but with the seasonal influx of summer traffic, it is probably also the fastest route. It is a magic journey, shifting from farm fields (corn and soybean) to forest canopy.

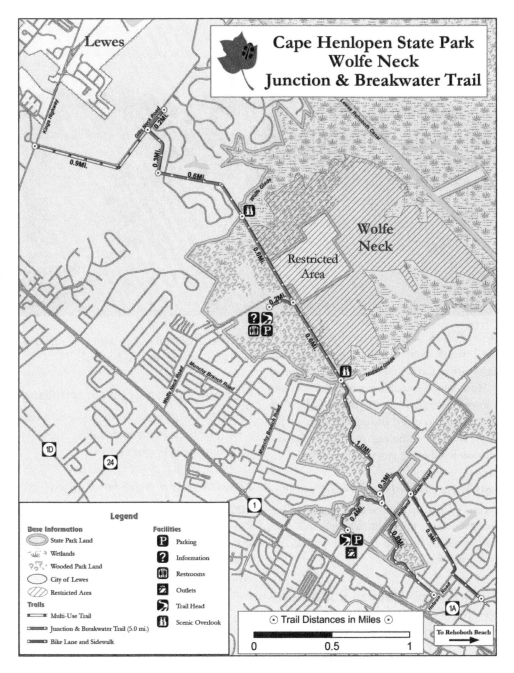

**Cape Henlopen State Park
Wolfe Neck
Junction & Breakwater Trail**

Legend

Base Information
- State Park Land
- Wetlands
- Wooded Park Land
- City of Lewes
- Restricted Area

Trails
- Multi-Use Trail
- Junction & Breakwater Trail (5.0 mi.)
- Bike Lane and Sidewalk

Facilities
- P — Parking
- ? — Information
- Restrooms
- Outlets
- Trail Head
- Scenic Overlook

⊙ Trail Distances in Miles ⊙

0   0.5   1

To Rehoboth Beach

This nearly 6 mile packed-earth, gravel and boardwalk off-road trail follows (and takes its name from) the railroad that dates back to 1878, when the line was extended from Lewes to the Methodist meeting grounds of Rehoboth (known then as Henlopen City).

The trail, consisting of finely crushed stone with an average width of 12 feet, includes an 80-foot long railroad bridge originally built in 1913, views of wetlands and a World War II observation tower.

Start your trip on the road at the traffic cir-

cle on Rehoboth Avenue and head west over the Lewes-Rehoboth Canal to make a sharp right turn at the stoplight on Church Street.

Turn left on Canal Street to pass by an area known as West Rehoboth, a traditionally black community founded during the days of Jim Crow laws. The stop sign at Canal Street and Hebron Road offers two choices.

Left Turn on Hebron Road will allow

cyclists to pick up the trailhead just after Burton Avenue on the right, where a split-level fence gives entrance to an enchanting section of forested trail.

Right Turn on Hebron Road leads on

open roadway past housing developments and the community of West Rehoboth.

From either alternative, trail users will

eventually reach Holland Glade Road where more options for continuing north on the trail present themselves.

Go straight across Holland

Glade Road to pick up the trail on farmland leading into the woods ahead.

Continuing east down Holland Glade Road is yet another option. Make

a left just before Rehoboth Little League to enter the wooded canopy of trail.

Now, for the next few miles, all sections of the trail go off-road.

On any given summer evening, a ball game may be in full swing just behind the tree line while around the corner, deer are feasting in the farmland adjacent to this forested canopy of hardwood conifers, hemlock and maple trees.

All the various sections of trail funnel into the same main corri-

dor. At this point, cyclists continue around the perimeter of farmland where soybeans flower and rows of corn silk in mid-summer. Turning off at the Wolfe Neck trailhead leads to a rest area with picnic tables and the Wolfe House, an old farmhouse (circa 1875) that has been preserved and restored.

Plate 108. Mary Wardencki Cottage 4 (3-34-13.20-81), From the East.

WEST REHOBOTH

The southwesterly trailhead of the Junction and Breakwater Trail leads cyclists and runners along Hebron Road, a main artery of the vibrant, traditionally black community of West Rehoboth.

"The folks of West Rehoboth were crab catchers, clam shuckers, dishwashers, waitresses, maids and lawn mowers," wrote novelist Alexs D. Pate, the author of *West of Rehoboth*. "They provided the human arms which kept the Rockwellian town bristling clean . . . And when they were done with their chores in Rehoboth Beach, they were remanded to the western province."

When Quaker Charles Mills returned from World War II to manage the Stokely cannery in Rehoboth Beach, Jim Crow laws were still in effect mandating separation of black and white neighborhoods. Mills, who would have great success as a farmer as well a corporate executive, set out to right a social wrong when he noticed that (the mostly black) employees in the cannery struggled to find housing. He parceled off a section of his personal land holdings and sold it to families to help provide fair housing for Rehoboth Beach (and workers for his enterprises).

"In 1945, I got out of the Army, Mr. Charlie Mills was selling land," recalled one long-time West Rehoboth resident Johnnie Cannon. "Before this, the land was all string beans. It was farmland. I bought two plots from Mr. Mills. For a lot 50-by-175 ft., I paid $100. The next one was $10 cheaper. He told me that if I wanted the rest of them all the way down, that I could have them for $70 a lot."

This enclave of some 200 residents, north of Rehoboth Avenue and west of the canal, housed much of the labor force of Rehoboth Beach. The community was once home to a variety of businesses that have long since disappeared, including the long-defunct Miss Edna's Restaurant and Dance Floor, the 400 Social Club and the edgier Do Drop Inn.

During the 1980s and 90's the neighborhood experienced problems due to drugs, crime, vacancy and absentee landlords. Over the last decade, though, the formation of a coalition to preserve the heritage of West Rehoboth has resulted in new, affordable housing. Plans to restore this tight-knit community, once known for its greenery and abundance of opportunity for African-Americans, include the installation of sidewalks, street lamps, a playground and more housing. ■

THE MAKING OF THE JUNCTION & BREAKWATER TRAIL

S usan Moerschel is widely credited for spearheading the development and construction of the Junction & Breakwater Trail while Manager of the Park Resource Office of the Delaware Department of Natural Resources & Environmental Control. Here is her recollection of the creation of the Breakwater trail:

"The idea of the trail was noted in a 1974 study, and a 1980 plan recommended the route along the Penn Central rail line stating ominously that it 'would be the easiest to construct and would have the least environmental impact, but... would require right-of-way acquisition from private owners.'

Our Department of Transportation (DelDOT), which conducted both studies, was not yet in the business of creating bike and pedestrian facilities. And there was neither the interest not the funding to justify land purchases by DelDOT or my Department (Delaware Division of Parks and Recreation).

As property values at the beach continued to rise, traffic grew too, as did the use of bicycles in the region. Our agency now had access to a steady and reliable source of land protection funds and a very long list of projects. Land purchases along the rail line had to wait their turn. Speaking to trail supporters, I impressed upon them the need to purchase land before it was devoured by sprawl. It was the trail's local supporters that convinced our Division's managers to protect lands between Lewes and Rehoboth, sooner rather than later.

Two stream corridors, wetlands, forests and fields, a few miles of that old Penn Central line and a 1938 railroad bridge were all part of the 1,500 acres now preserved. When Governor Ruth Ann Minner announced our land protection successes, she said a trail would be built and it would be built of stone.

On a chilly November day in 2003, Phase I of the dream was complete. In the middle of the trail, next to Lt. Governor Carney, stood folks who were once opposed, long-time trail supporters, new and former legislators, construction managers, and trail users. Someone remarked that day that trail users are friendly and warm. Imagine that! That's quite a difference from the long-ago worries of bad trouble on trails and bad things happening to neighborhoods near the trail." ∎

AN ALTERNATIVE WAY BACK VIA GORDON'S POND

Returning to Rehoboth is as easy as making a u-turn and retracing the trail. But another alternative is also available for the trip back through Cape Henlopen State Park past wonderful Gordon's Pond.

At the corner of Gill's Neck and the main Lewes thoroughfare of Savannah Road, turn right (over the bridge). Just before Savannah Road ends at Lewes Beach, make a right on Cape Henlopen Drive (Dairy Queen) and proceed straight to enter the state park. Ask the gate attendant for a map leading to the Gordon Pond bike path which will take you past dunes and World War II surveillance towers, along the edge of the pond, and finally back to Rehoboth Beach.

A new trail, at the cost of over a million dollars, opened in 2014 and was an immediate hit.

● ●

Across Wolf Neck Road the trail opens into more forestry and then over the marshes that serve as incubators for young wildlife and waterfowl. The views of wildlife and the estuary at-work are not to be missed; interpretive signage will help identify some of the most common.

Eventually, the trail will deliver users into the southernmost parts of Lewes and the community of Hawkseye, which features a paved median throughway at the end of the trail on the residential Golden Eagle Boulevard. Turning right on the perpendicular Peregrine Road offers an exit from the trail leading to Gills Neck Road but continuing straight along the median will bring cyclists into the neighboring community of Senators, which also exits on Gills Neck Road.

A left turn on Gills Neck Road will take trail users to Cape Henlopen High School along a trailway bordered by split rail fence on one side and Gills Neck Road on the other.

A right on Gills Neck Road leads riders and runners into downtown Lewes with a view of the Lewes-Rehoboth Canal along the way. ■

Gay Rehoboth

HE SAID, SHE SAID:
REHOBOTH'S GAY HISTORY

By Rich Barnett and Fay Jacobs

Writers and raconteurs Rich Barnett and Fay Jacobs recount the emergence of Rehoboth's gay and lesbian community in a dual-focused dialogue.

Fay: Sapphic Beginnings

Lore has it that Rehoboth's gay history begins with DuPont heiress Louisa Carpenter, a lesbian who carried on a longtime affair with torch singer Libby Holman. Louisa hunted fox and pheasant, raised horses, and was one of the first licensed woman pilots. She entertained actress and bon vivant Tallulah Bankhead and other gay and bisexual theatre and Hollywood friends at the family's summer home on Silver Lake just south of the Boardwalk in the 1930s and early 1940s.

As much as I love to think it was Louisa and Tallulah who put Rehoboth on the gay radar, I think it might have been the reputation of Rehoboth as an art colony in the 1920s and 1930s that began to draw gays and lesbians. The Rehoboth Art League was established in 1938 by a very dedicated and close-knit group of Delaware artists and arts patrons, mostly women, some of whom were rumored to be "sapphically-inclined."

Louisa Carpenter

Rich: The Quiet Years

By the 1950s, so many Washingtonians were spending their summers in Rehoboth that the town was known as The Nation's Summer Capital, a nickname it still maintains today. The opening of the Chesapeake Bay Bridge in 1952 made it easier than ever for Washingtonians to visit Rehoboth. Gay men and women joined this summer migration. By the 50s, there was a small but growing social network of closeted Washingtonians visiting Rehoboth and even starting to buy houses. The fact that Rehoboth didn't have the gay reputation of Provincetown and Fire Island was considered as a good thing.

The 50s weren't a good time to be gay and lesbian. President Eisenhower issued an executive order in 1953 barring gay men and lesbians from all federal jobs. Many state and local governments and private corporations followed suit. The FBI began a surveillance program against homosexuals.

It's no wonder that gay life in Rehoboth during the 50s and early 60s was quiet. Most socializing revolved around swank cocktail and dinner parties in private homes. And though there were no gay bars per se, there were a few with "reputations," including the Bottle and Cork in Dewey and the Pink Pony in Rehoboth. The bar at the Dinner Bell Inn was supposedly gay one night per week.

I've been told back then gays and lesbians gathered on the beach at the end of Olive and

Virginia Streets — very near the Pink Pony. The Pleasant Inn, in the house that now stands at the corner of Olive and Second Streets, had a word of mouth reputation as a gay-friendly establishment. It had been in the Ocean block of Virginia Street before it was moved. Peck Pleasanton, the somewhat closeted gay owner of the Inn, and his mother, were known for their cocktail hour with guests. I've even heard that his mother preferred to rent to gay men because she didn't get any trouble out of them.

The Opening of the Bay Bridge, 1952

Fay: Game Changers

In 1960, a man named Randall Godwin and his wife Betty opened The Nomad Village, a package store and bar just south of Dewey Beach in an isolated location on the highway. Bartender Jimmy Short suggested opening a back bar that catered to gays and lesbians, as more and more gays were visiting the Delaware shore. Word spread that the Nomad was a great meeting spot for gay folk. The couple later added hotel rooms for rent. The Nomad operated, mostly as a gay bar, until it closed in the late '90s – with Jimmy at the bar

until the very end.

Another couple – Ross Alexander and his partner Fran Heuber – opened and ran Joss Gift Store on Rehoboth Avenue in 1964. It is believed to be Rehoboth's first gay-owned business.

On July 4, 1973, Wilmingon, Delaware bar owner Francis Murphy joined a straight couple named Sid and June Sennebaum to open the Boathouse on the bay in Dewey Beach. Patrons recall it as a low-slung, white frame building patrolled for safety by beefy, straight bouncers from the University of Delaware football team. Besides a dance floor able to accommodate a large disco crowd, there was, at the rear of the building a second bar with a bank of open windows overlooking a dock and the bay. It wasn't air conditioned, and at high tide the rear bar would frequently flood, which added to the fes-

BALTIMORE AVENUE

"Those coming to Rehoboth for the first time will find that the gayest block in town is Baltimore Avenue. There you can eat breakfast, lunch and dinner; do your shopping; and go to happy hour and late-night dancing all on the same block, with nearly all the businesses owned and operated by members of the LGBT community. You can stop by CAMP, the Rehoboth LGBT Community Center, and get all the information you need for a great weekend or the whole summer."

Peter D. Rosenstein, HuffPost Gay Voices

TOP TEN THINGS TO DO IN REHOBOTH

Fay's Top 5

- Spend a day at Gordon's Pond beach at Cape Henlopen State Park. It's where the girls are.
- Enjoy a cocktail with everyone's favorite mixologist Ginger at the bar at MIXX Restaurant on Baltimore Avenue.
- A night out listening and dancing wherever Vickie Dee is performing.
- Visit Proud Bookstore on Baltimore Avenue. It's one of the few remaining LGBT bookstores in the country.
- Stop in at the CAMP Rehoboth Community Center, pick up a copy of LETTERS and have lunch at Lori's café in the courtyard. You'll find out about everything going on in town.

Rich's Top 5

- Spend a day at Poodle Beach at the height of the season. Grab a flavorful frozen ice from the Planet Ice concession, sit back, and enjoy the eye candy and antics on one of the country's top gay beaches.
- Go for happy hour al fresco at Aqua on Baltimore Avenue. Cocktails taste better when served by handsome shirtless waiters.
- Check out the annual sandcastle contest just north of the Boardwalk. Go early and watch how they build 'em — it's both a science and an art. Enter if you dare...
- Hop on a bicycle and explore Rehoboth's quaint neighborhoods. Check out all the unique house names, a Rehoboth tradition
- Come for the fall. The crowds are gone but the gays are still here. The beach is de lightful, and all the shops and restaurants are still open for business.

tivities. It was the area's first true gay bar and dance club and it attracted a lot of people and a lot of attention, until it burned down mysteriously a few years after opening.

Rich: Out of the Shadows

The gay migration to Rehoboth continued, fueled mainly by word of mouth among the burgeoning gay populations in Washington, Baltimore, Philadelphia, and Wilmington. It was a new era of gay pride, disco, coming out, and increased activism following the assassination of Harvey Milk in San Francisco and the anti-gay tirades of Anita Bryant in Florida.

Another factor might have been the decline of Atlantic City as a gay beach destination. When the gambling casinos came in, they displaced a lot of that city's gay bars and motels. Consequently, a lot of guys in the Mid-Atlantic region who used to go to Atlantic City began going to Rehoboth.

The first article in the Washington *Blade* (that city's gay newspaper) touting Rehoboth as a gay vacation destination appeared in 1978. Sun, sand, surf, sex, and sociability — that's the picture of Rehoboth painted by the author. By the late 70s, hundreds of gays were congregating each weekend on the beach just south of the Boardwalk in front of the Carpenter estate — the exact spot where Louisa and her friends used to frolic back in the 1930's. Gay guys were also frequenting the beach at Gordon's Pond, as it had developed a quiet reputation as a place for au naturel sun worship without any hassles. There were a lot of dunes back then, two rows in fact, and plenty of cover for cruising and sex.

In May 1980, a Washington gay bar owner/operator named Glen Thompson opened The Renegade Dance Club, beside a cornfield on Route One just outside downtown Rehoboth. Thompson knew the time was right for such an establishment in Rehoboth. Eight weeks later it burned to the ground. Thompson, though, re-built and the Renegade evolved into a major gay destination, known throughout the Mid-Atlantic for its disco floor and drag shows. Thompson later added a pool and motel units.

A year later, restaurant entrepreneurs Victor

Pisapia and Joyce Felton opened the Blue Moon on Baltimore Avenue. Despite the excellent food reviews from the *New York Times* and *Gourmet Magazine*, many in Rehoboth weren't ready for such a visible gay presence right in the heart of town. The anti-gay backlash was beginning. Meetings were held, sides were drawn, and it wasn't unusual for the restaurant to be pelted with tomatoes or beer bottles from passing cars. Just as Joyce and Victor were frightened by the reactions the Blue Moon unleashed, so too were townsfolk frightened by this new constituency they didn't understand.

The harassment and threats continued for years, but the customers kept coming. In addition to the loyal regulars, gay and straight, who savored the Blue Moon for its sophisticated food and ambiance, high profile people like Frank Purdue, Baltimore Oriole Jim Palmer, Congressman Barney Frank, and Governor Tom Carper dined at the Moon.

Rehoboth's Mayor at the time exacerbated the issue by speaking out to journalists about the town's "gay problem" and the damage to its reputation. Of course not all straight folk in Rehoboth shared the Mayor's sentiments. Many recognized that gays were good for business and brought an air of sophistication and fine dining to compete with the crab houses and pizza joints. Many say the Mayor's antics put Rehoboth even more on the gay radar.

In 1988 a disco named The Strand opened on Rehoboth Avenue, turning a shuttered movie house into a hot nightspot. Weekends found up to 700 gay men and lesbians dancing under disco glitter balls long into the night. But every time the Strand applied for a liquor license, the Rehoboth Homeowner's Association drew a line in the sand, using noise, traffic, and parking concerns to bolster their pleas for denial. But underneath the arguments, was the real reason for the opposition – the Strand catered to homosexuals. Sadly for all its fans, the Strand could not survive the lack of a liquor license as well as the growing anti-gay sentiment in town.

Fay: Acceptance

With gays and lesbians being much more visible in town by the early 1990s, many residents feared their town was being overtaken. Bumper stickers appeared saying "Keep Rehoboth a Family Town" and there were some terrible gay-bashing incidents. Something needed to be done to bring the gay and straight communities together.

In this toxic environment, two gay men – Steve Elkins and Murray Archibald – launched a new nonprofit organization with a mission of bringing the gay and straight communities together. They called it CAMP Rehoboth. CAMP being an acronym for Create A More Positive Rehoboth, a nod to the gay community's hallmark campiness, the founding of Rehoboth as a Methodist camp meeting, and the biblical interpretation of Rehoboth meaning "room for all."

CAMP Rehoboth volunteers began hosting meetings with local government officials, conducting sensitivity training with the police department, and interacting with homeowner associations to try to bring the diverse communities closer. The new positive approach began working. In the late 90s, Rehoboth experienced a real estate boom, a force that united gays and straights in the mutual quest for nice houses, a nice community, and nice profits. By 2010, an editorial in the *Wilmington News Journal* credited Rehoboth's gay community as being one of the leading factors in Rehoboth weathering 2009's national great recession.

In 2003, Rehoboth Beach added sexual orientation to its anti-discrimination ordinance (housing, employment, public works contracting, and public accommodations). It was passed unanimously and was the first such ordinance passed in Delaware.

Now in Rehoboth Beach and the surrounding areas there is a huge gay population, many gay and lesbian owed and operated businesses and a throng of gay visitors seamlessly blending with the community at large. There are gay and lesbian City commissioners, and it is often hard to tell whether a business is gay or straight-owned. Pretty much, everyone is welcome anywhere.

In a symbolic gesture, the signing of the bill that added the words "sexual orientation" to the Delaware non-discrimination law took place at CAMP Rehoboth in Rehoboth Beach in 2009. By 2012, Delaware had added Civil Unions and then Marriage Equality to the law and Rehoboth became is prime location for GLBT weddings.

Rehoboth today is touted as one of America's best gay beaches. It's also annointed as one of the country's top retirement destinations. It's a great mix. ∎

CONVERSATION: STEVE ELKINS
Executive Director, CAMP Rehoboth

CAMP REHOBOTH

Atlanta native Steve Elkins worked in the Jimmy Carter Presidency, serving for three years in the White House Office of Administration. "From my days in Washington," he recalls, "I learned that if you believe in what you're doing, put aside all the naysayers, and stay true to your mission, you'd be surprised at what you can accomplish." He and his partner Murray Archibald started CAMP Rehoboth in 1991 as a focus for the growing gay and lesbian population and to provide a forum for the entire Rehoboth Beach community.

"My partner Murray Archibald and I were living in New York, where I was the district sales manager for a computer company. We had been coming to Rehoboth for years. On Friday we'd get on the 5 o'clock Metroliner at Penn Station and be in Rehoboth by 8:20. We'd go back Monday morning and I'd be in the office by noon. I was taking my vacations a half-day at a time.

Then PCs were introduced, the bottom fell out of the computer business. In 1990 we moved down to Rehoboth full-time. By then,

Rehoboth was on the summer weekend map amongst the gay community in D.C. and Baltimore. I ran two restaurants and then a dance club, The Strand, which we helped design and was owned by the people who owned the Blue Moon restaurant.

The Strand was really a major turning point in the history of Rehoboth. It was an after-hour dance club. It also had an 'under 21 club' for kids. We never got a liquor license so we were really strict about not allowing drinking. Everybody was checked at the door. The owner of an out-of-town club once asked if we were looking for weapons and I answered 'no, we're looking for beer!'

The opening of the Strand was a galvanizing moment. The club was on Rehoboth Avenue and the prospect of crowds of gays lining the sidewalk on the main street in town upset some people. Homophobia raised its head. Carloads of teen-age boys would drive around and throw rocks; a crew went into the Blue Moon and ripped the sink off the wall.

Bumper stickers started showing up distributed by the Homeowner's Association that read 'Keep Rehoboth a Family Town.' That's what got Murray and me going. We wanted Rehoboth to be a family town, too, but we believed that family's come in all sizes and shapes. The Mayor of Rehoboth at the time was John Hughes. He would say a few years later, after the community started coming together, that the right bumper sticker should have been 'Keep Rehoboth Diverse'.

That was the origins of CAMP Rehoboth. Our idea was to develop an organization that would let people get together to talk. There was a new resurgence in the community, gays and lesbians were more willing to be open. There were storeowners at the time, for example, who were very gay but wouldn't admit to it. We started saying it should be just the opposite, that we should be celebrating diversity as a great boon to the economy.

There was a horrific gay bashing incident at the south end of the boardwalk in 1992 that ended up galvanizing the town. Around one o'clock on a Sunday morning, four gay men were sitting on a bench talking. A group of five out-of-towners, who hadn't been able to find the party they were looking for, came upon them and picked a fight. One of the men was bashed with a baseball bat, another got hit over the head with an empty bottle of champagne so severely that it was feared he would never regain his faculties.

The new police chief, Craig Doyle, came over to CAMP Rehoboth and said 'I'm not going to tolerate this in my town.' The city officials and the Chamber of Commerce wanted to sweep the incident under the table to hide the terrible publicity. But Doyle said 'we're gong to have zero tolerance and we're going to talk about it.' I went on the air and to the media. The city officials agreed we were right.

The attackers were arrested. I sat through the entire trial. One of them, 15 years old, was being brought up by his grandparents and his grandmother said 'we have not raised him to hate and to have prejudice.' That was a seminal moment for me. I realized that what we had to do was reach out, that kids were being taught to hate even if they weren't raised that way. It was a blessing in disguise that I got to see all that.

That year, 1992, we did training for the police to help them understand what this 'new' community was about. I've continued to do this every year since. The essential message is that, regardless of anybody's personal opinion, when they put on a uniform we expect that they will treat everybody the same. In the beginning I'd ask 'do any of you know somebody who is gay?' and they'd cross their arms in front of their chest and stare back blankly. Several years ago, to show how things have changed, two raised their hands and said 'I'm gay' and a third said 'I'm not gay but I've got two mothers.'

Rehoboth is different from other places like Provincetown or Key West. We're a much more integrated community, gay and straight. CAMP Rehoboth has prided itself on not only being a non-separatist organization for gay but non-separatist for heterosexual. There were some who thought we should be more partisan, like ACT UP. But that's never been our vision. We see ourselves as an umbrella organization that figures out ways for everybody to work together." ∎

A TONY BURNS PORTFOLIO

Since Tony Burns started coming to Rehoboth Beach in the late 1970s, he has been photographing events and gatherings. Some two-dozen albums of his pictures over the years are permanently shelved at CAMP Rehoboth, documenting the gay male scene. "I never would have dreamed that we would have the community that we have today when I first came here. What we've done here is mainstream the gays and straights together in a way that doesn't exist elsewhere, there just isn't any other place in the country that can measure up to this."

Art League &
Henlopen Acres

HENLOPEN ACRES

What Henlopen Acres may lack in size, it more than makes up for in charm, leafy ambiance, and access to the water.

Since 1970, it has been an incorporated town, one of the smallest in the state consisting of less than one-third of a square mile. Only about one-third of the homes in Henlopen Acres are lived in year-round; the rest are vacation homes or rental properties.

But those 123 acres make for a pricey neighborhood, with houses priced in the millions.

Henlopen Acres is tied with Greenville, home of the DuPont estates, as having the highest personal incomes in the state, with a median household income of $130,000.

Henlopen Acres was developed by Colonel Wilbur S. Corkran, who purchased a 156-acre parcel of farmland in 1931 for $100,000. He and his wife, Louise, had moved into the area several years earlier, living in the historic house that sits on the grounds of what is now the Rehoboth Art League. He parceled his holdings into more than 200 lots, promoting the estates to "quiet-loving, cultured people."

The original development included a riding academy and yacht basin, and property owners are still eligible to join the Henlopen Acres Beach Club. ■

THE RHOBOTH ART LEAGUE

The Rehoboth Art League harkens back to an earlier era when artist colonies spouted up amidst an American landscape largely indifferent to culture.

Its origins date to Wilbur Corkran, a Maryland native who earned an engineering degree from the University of Delaware, served as a Colonel with the Army Corps of Engineers, then started a company specializing in railroad tunnel construction. In 1929, he and his wife Louise Chambers, one of the country's first professionally trained interior designers (their house and garden in Short Hills, NJ was featured in the *New York Times*), bought the historic Peter Marsh house and

farm. Within several years, he had established an architectural practice in Rehoboth and was heading up the Delaware Mosquito Control Commission.

The couple had grand ambitions—both artistic and commercial—-for their new homestead. He began at once to market lots for a development to be called Henlopen Acres, described in its original sales brochure as a community where "cultured people" would live "amid conditions which make for health, comfort, and refined pleasure." Preeminent among those 'refined pleasures' was to be a center for the arts, driven forward through the enthusiasm of Mrs. Corkran.

By the spring of 1937, she had brought together some two-dozen local women to plan for an art league. They began selling Delaware-made pottery to raise funds. An abandoned two-room farmhouse a few miles away was floated down the Lewes-Rehoboth Canal and mounted on two acres of land lent by the Colonel to house the first artists' studio. More than two hundred people gathered in June 1938 to officially dedicate the Rehoboth Art League. By that summer, classes were being offered along with Sunday afternoon teas to invite the public to view exhibitions.

Expansion followed World War II as the Corkran Building was added, for exhibition and teaching space. Artists were attracted to the beauty of the grounds. More facilities were added, including an art library. A permanent collection was steadily acquired. The Clothesline Show, named because art works were strung on conventional clotheslines to be exhibited, debuted in 1941. The gardens were restored to resemble their colonial origins, a Children's Studio opened in 2002.

In 1970, Henlopen Acres was charted as an independent town, complete with its own government and post office (as well as a beach, marina, and horseback riding school). The Corkran Homestead served as the centerpiece of the community, its 'public common.' Upon the death of Mrs. Corkran, it was deeded (with Art League facilities) to the University of Delaware but it quickly became apparent that the University was unable to adequately maintain the grounds and historic structures. In 1979, ownership of the facility was transferred to the Rehoboth Art League. ■

League Founder Louise Corkran having her portrait painted

'MY ABILITY TO DO SOMETHING TOWARD THIS END'

"The idea of a summer art school and exhibitions in Rehoboth is owing in large part to the local women's club, the Village Improvement Association, which for the preceding eight or ten years had staged a summer art exhibition ... My ability to do something toward this end had its genesis years ago when I spent a vacation in Bethany Beach and Rehoboth. Born and reared in Kentucky, it was in Rehoboth that I met my future husband and in Lewes that I first heard of the Art School in Philadelphia which I later attended ....

From the beginning in 1938, when the league had but eight members, $25 given me by a sorority sister's father, and a kitchen wing of an antique farm house bought for $15.00 (no widows, no doors, no roof, no floors), it has now developed into an organization of nearly one thousand members from Maine to Florida, as well as South Africa and Indonesia, with five studios in three buildings."

Louise C. Corkran
1970

Art League & Henlopen Acres
Conversation: Sheila Bravo
Executive Director, Rehoboth Art League

In the midst of a corporate career in brand management and global business development, Sheila Bravo realized on her son's third birthday that "for his entire life, he had only seen me on weekends. That wasn't what I wanted." She converted herself into a consultant, earning a Ph.D. specializing in the governance of non-profits.

"I live in Lewes, where my husband is the Rector at St. Peter's. I learned about the Art League when my son participated in their Young Art Program. When the previous director left, I put my name in for the job and got it.

Art grows here in Rehoboth and Sussex County. The mission of the Art League is all about connecting people to those arts. Our role is to inspire people to make art, to offer classes (more than one hundred), to mount exhibitions and host events like the annual outdoor show.

Artist communities—-potters, open studios and sketch groups, writers groups—-work out of the League.

Our cultural imperative is outreach, insuring that experiencing the arts is accessible in both price and location. The physical imperative is preservation, showcasing the heritage of the artists who have created the League and inspiring a new generation. Our campus is an extraordinary asset with three historic buildings over 200 years old; the Homestead is on the National Register of Historic Places. Even though the League's balance sheet is healthy, it's a challenge to keep pace with the immense amount of repairs and maintenance the campus requires.

We've conducted an entire campus assessment with a five-year maintenance and upgrade plan. At the same time we're looking at more outreach into the community. And we have a collection of some one

thousand works to maintain. All together, that's some fairly big activities.

Our location poses a challenge with respect to outreach. It is difficult for much of the residential population to navigate through the heavy in-season traffic to the campus in Henlopen Acres. Many residents don't even know we're here. We're exploring the idea of satellite facilities to make it much easier to access our resources. Our experiment with a temporary gallery on Rehoboth Avenue (thanks to the generosity of the landlord) is a test for us to learn what it takes to have such sites around the area. People love to stop by and look at art. It's remarkable how many come in and say they didn't even know the League existed.

What makes non-profit governance unique is that, unlike in the private sector where the C.E.O. and the board are accountable to the owners of the company, in a non-profit we're responsible to the community. In effect, the community is overseeing the operation.

Sussex County and the coastal side of Delaware are waiting for an inclusive Center of the Arts that would allow the various cultural organizations here to be able to grow and thrive. The talent of the individuals moving here brings a wealth of skill and expertise that they are eager to contribute to the community. As one of the leading arts organizations in the state, the Art League can serve as a leader in that kind of conversation.

The next piece in building a vibrant climate is to increase collaboration amongst the different organizations like the League, the Rehoboth Film Society and Coastal Concerts. When you partner and collaborate, you can share experiences and it makes everybody stronger. ■

THE HOMESTEAD

The Homestead is a cypress shingled house built around 1742 by Peter Marsh, who had bought a tract of land called Young's Hope. Marsh, according to legend, chose this location to settle in order to easily search for the pirate gold he believed was buried nearby in the dunes.

The walls of the old wing and interior partitions are filled with brick in the manner of the day. The framing is of hand-hewn walnut instead of the usual oak. Hand-made doors, primitive paneling on the chimneybreasts, and wide floorboards were carefully preserved by Col. Corkran, who followed the original style in additions.

The formal garden is a show-place of the county. By tradition, the well on the front slope is a 'wishing well,' sought in past times by young couples to make their vows to each other." ∎

HOWARD PYLE: REHOBOTH'S 'ARTIST OF THE ROMANTIC ROGUE

The most celebrated artist to reside locally was Howard Pyle, whose family owned a cottage in the Pines from the turn-of-the-twentieth century. Here he spent summers and attracted other high caliber artists to join him.

Pyle was among the first rank of American magazine and book illustrators of his era, particularly famed for his contributions to medieval youth sagas. *The Merry Adventures of Robin Hood*, his first success, prompted one critic to accuse him of replacing reality with romance: "He altered the protagonist from a selfish, murdering crook into a philanthropist who robs the rich and gives to the poor." No matter, Robin Hood would be henceforth 'branded' as a hero of the people.

His rendering of pirates similarly created their prototype as elegant villains. Although there was no evidence of what pirates wore, his drawings established a flamboyant, romantic style that continues today. Think of Johnny Depp's Jack Sparrow character, who is 100% Pyle.

Pyle was also founder of the famed Brandywine School in Pennsylvania where he mentored, among others, N.C. Wyeth, noted in his own right and the father of American icon Andrew Wyeth.

Pyle died in 1911. The Art League's dedication ceremonies in 1938 were very much in homage to him, with his widow (who lived in Rehoboth Beach), honored as the first signer of the first Door of Fame. ∎

REHOBOTH
Dining

So many restaurants, so little time! Numerous restaurant associations and the prestigious James Beard Foundation have recognized our chefs and restaurateurs as outstanding.

So where's a good place to eat? Since 2009, the Rehoboth Foodie tells it like it is with honest reviews, commentary, photos of local cuisine and the latest news on restaurant specials, happy hours and charity events. Check out RehobothFoodie.com for the highlights and lowdown on the business of eating in the Rehoboth Beach area.

Cape Gazette restaurant columnist Bob Yesbek reports on the best local pizza. There are some who whisper that he could also be the Rehoboth Foodie, who describes Five Great Rehoboth Eating Experiences and reviews downtown restaurants, but the Foodie never comes out from behind that hamburger long enough for anyone to be sure.

photography by Bob Yesbek

FIVE GREAT REHOBOTH BEACH DINING EXPERIENCES

by Bob Yesbek

I've assembled five great meals at five of Rehoboth's best restaurants. Fair warning, though: Menus change with the season, so some of these dishes might not be available when you go. But don't let that stop you: Use this as a guideline, because you can't go wrong at these five delightful eateries.

a(MUSE.)

a(MUSE.) is anything but your typical restaurant. Owner/chef (and James Beard nominee) Hari Cameron is proving beyond a doubt that serious diners are ready for his daring gastronomy.

The menu is divided into Firsts, Seconds, Tastings and Finale. Firsts contains his legendary small-plate *objets d'art*, and my favorite is the poached lobster with carrot puree, lacto-fermented and shattered carrots (think liquid nitrogen!), lobster roe, bibb hearts and foraged rose hips. The generous portion of lobster includes a meaty knuckle or two, and is a light and cool way to jump-start your adventure.

Another dish worthy of a MOMA exposition is the potato cream soup which Cameron decorates with hen o' the woods mushrooms, pine nut crumbs (there's that nitrogen again), charred & pickled onions and locally foraged pine salt. Soothing to eat. Beautiful to behold.

For Seconds I never miss the Dogfish Ale-infused pâte à choux gnocchi. It plays politely on the plate with caramelized brussels sprouts, turnips 3-ways, crispy sage in sage brown butter and shaved Granny Smith apples drizzled with paprika honey. The gnocchi are like tiny creampuffs scented with hops and grain, and their yielding texture, paired with the tartness of the apples, sets off a party in your mouth. ■

BRAMBLE & BRINE

In the late fall of 2013, Joe and Megan Churchman restored the iconic Rehoboth Avenue structure that had been home to South Pacific Florist for over 26 years, adding a kitchen as big as some in-town eateries, but remaining true to the cottage's turn-of-the-century charm.

No visit is complete without one of the rare items that has remained on the appetizer menu since they opened: The rib eye crown with roasted red onion & sweet corn sauté, red wine verjus watercress coulis. There's just enough succulent, perfectly to-temperature steak to sat-

isfy that craving – while still leaving room for the cool and crunchy chestnut smoked ricotta salad with beets, cucumbers, pea tendrils, micro basil and bread & butter pickle dressing.

Bramble & Brine is a haven for carnivores, so the thing to do is go ahead and order the brown sugar and spice-brined Berkshire pork chop. It's so tender you can cut it with a fork as it rests happily on a bed of hominy (corn kernels that have been soaked in an alkaline solution that causes the grain to puff up to twice its normal size). The pork chop is crowned with crispy herbs drizzled in a Madeira reduction. ∎

CONFUCIUS

Say "Chinese food," and the first thought that comes to mind is probably "sweet and sour something-or-the-other" that's been sitting on a steam table all day.

But that's not the case at Confucius Chinese Cuisine in Rehoboth Beach. Owners Shawn and Danielle Xiong were born in Hunan Province, China. They love the food they grew up with, and they take it seriously. "Our recipes are for those who want to go a step further in their enjoyment of Chinese Food," says Shawn.

The appetizer menu is a journey through taste, texture and temperature. Start with the spicy cold noodles. The contrast between the Sriracha-borne garlic/pepper heat and the cool al dente noodles will keep you coming back. Salt & pepper shrimp share that spotlight. But the salt & pepper calamari steals the show. Rather than being cut into the classic rings, a briny, spice-infused batter encases the entire mantle (the tubular body) which is then fried to a crisp finish. It's like eating a crunchy Popsicle with a cephalopod surprise inside.

My favorite main course is Kung Pao Chicken: Firm, brightly colored vegetables and crackly peanuts bask in a savory, semi-opaque sauce, aromatic with red and white peppers. If you're nice, they'll mix shrimp and chicken for your Kung Pao. It's a roller coaster of shapes and texture, and worth every penny. ■

BACK PORCH CAFÉ

Not only is Back Porch Café one of the very best fine-dining restaurants in Rehoboth Beach, it is also the oldest (2014 marks their fortieth year anniversary). The casual beach-house setting belies some of the best French cuisine in the state. Years ago when I first interviewed the late Chef/co-owner Leo Medisch, he made Back Porch Café's mission very clear: "You've got to be willing to spend the money for the very best ingredients," he said. "You can't save pennies when it comes to specialty meats, fresh fish, local produce, spices and quality olive oil." Staples like ketchup, salsa, preserved lemons, sausage, ravioli, rhubarb jam and even the restaurant's renowned desserts are made entirely in-house.

One of my favorite meals in Rehoboth Beach is the Sunday Brunch at Back Porch. It is absolutely necessary that you start with the blueberry scones. When most people are slathering butter on their morning pastries, at Back Porch Café you are slathering mascarpone cheese, preferably on the upper porch deck under the flowering Catalpa tree. And eggs Benedict are a must-get: Silky hollandaise covers perfectly poached eggs and savory Canadian bacon. There are no words.

Thirty-eight year veteran bartender Bee Neild's Flaming Coffee is another Rehoboth staple, and it's just as much fun to watch him make them as they are to sip. Using an open flame, cinnamon and spices are melted onto the rim of a goblet full of spicy coffee that has been spiked with a secret combination of spirits. ■

BLUE MOON

Blue Moon has been synonymous with quality dining and nightly partying for well over 30 years. No visit to Rehoboth can be complete without the Blue Moon experience.

The restaurant operations are overseen by co-owners Lion and Meg Gardner. The classically trained Lion is known for his whimsical menus and special events, none the least of which Tasting Tuesdays (wine flights paired with … it's always a surprise) and the popular Sunday Brunch. The meal I have created for you is a fantasy combination of both, as menus change like the wind here at the beach.

As you peruse the menu, Blue Moon's signature amuse bouche of roasted fig, gorgonzola and bacon arrives at your table. Making an entire meal out of these delightful morsels that light up every taste bud is #1 on my bucket list. If the stars are aligned correctly, fried oyster sliders will be on the menu. Plump, perfectly fried and spiced, the little bivalves peek out from soft, freshly made rolls. Keep repeating to yourself, "I must share this dish!" Because there's more to come.

So who in the world deep fries a soft-boiled egg? Chef Lion, of course. The crispy egg over bacon and red pepper hash is quite possibly one of the most delicious dishes to be had in Rehoboth Beach: a crunchy outside surrounding a still-runny yolk that flavors the savory bed of hash. My small-plate adventure at Blue Moon continues with the fried green tomatoes. The spicy crust is perfectly cooked and protects the firm surprise inside. The stack of three is perched squarely atop a bed of sweetly caramelized onions.

Blue Moon is known for desserts. The yuzu (a Japanese citrus fruit that resembles a small grapefruit but tastes more like a kafir lime) & pistachio icebox pie is the perfect foil for the savory dishes. But then there's also the crème brûlée! The dark and crunchy top protects some of the best vanilla crème you have ever tasted. Order both. Life is short. ∎

DOWNTOWN REHOBOTH RESTAURANTS

By The Rehoboth Foodie

$$$$ TOP OF THE LINE:

Back Porch Café
59 Rehoboth Avenue
302-227-3674
www.backporchcafe.com
This grande dame of Rehoboth Beach cuisine celebrates 40 years of upscale French dining served in a casual setting graced with creations by local artists. Executive chef Tim McNitt modifies the menu regularly depending on what's growing, flying or swimming out there.

In-season Sunday brunches at the Back Porch are the stuff of legend, and reservations are a must, especially if you wish to dine on the multi-tiered back porch. Don't miss the famous Flaming Coffee.

Blue Moon
35 Baltimore Avenue
302-227-6515
bluemoonrehoboth.com
When restaurants in Rehoboth grow up, they want to be the Blue Moon.

After more than 33 years, this fine-dining icon offers two distinct experiences in one bright blue and yellow Victorian mansion: First, the restaurant: Chef Lion Gardner's whimsical menu that's never without a surprise (southern-fried sweetbreads come to mind…), Tasting Tuesdays and a spectacular Sunday Brunch are the places to see and be seen.

Second, the Blue Moon bar: glitter, glamour, music, shirtless barkeeps and drag shows! Though the bar caters primarily to boys who like boys, it remains the center of upbeat Rehoboth nightlife for fun lovers of all persuasions.

a(MUSE.)
44 Rehoboth Avenue
302-227-7107
www.amuse-rehoboth.com
Delaware Restaurateur of the Year award winner Hari Cameron departs from the ordinary with handcrafted plates born of fresh, local ingredients and skillfully applied molecular gastronomy. Cameron's signature small plates are available individually, but foodies-in-the-know order the 7- or 11-course flights. The truly adventurous give Hari free rein to surprise them with delectable surprises that double as fine art.

a(MUSE.) is a late-night haven for chefs, food folk and those who love them. The Tuesday through Sunday late-night tasting menu kicks in at 9 p.m. at the bar and on the intimate candlelit patio.

a(MUSE.) is a one-of-a-kind experience and reservations are a must.

Bramble & Brine
315 Rehoboth Avenue
302-227-7702
www.brambleandbrine.com
Co-owner and Executive Chef Joey Churchman is a man of few words but lots of surprises. There's always something new, and his artistry with duck and unusual charcuterie is a closely guarded secret among Rehoboth's gastronomic cognoscenti.

Joey's wife Megan has outfitted the restaurant with collectibles and tchotchkes that she says are for sale, but may not be – depending on how attached to them she is. And that's the charm of Bramble & Brine: You never know exactly what you might experience.

Reservations shorten your wait, and you can pass the time at the white marble bar sipping a Churchmanhattan and weighing the vagaries of artisanal infusions with mixologist Rob Bagley.

Eden
23 Baltimore Avenue
302-227-3330
www.edenrestaurant.com
There is romance on the ocean block of Baltimore Avenue, and its name is Eden. Reserve the fabric-draped booths or 2nd floor balcony tables for a romantic dinner with candles flickering playfully off the walls. The menu changes regularly, but you can always rely on a good selection from chicken to veal to scallops to tuna. Chef Andrew Feeley has helped to set the fine dining standard in downtown Rehoboth bolstered by the 'beach-chic' dining room and in-season outdoor seating.

Delaware Today magazine proclaims Eden to be Most Romantic Atmosphere, and The Wine Spectator awards on the wall attest to the well-crafted list for which Eden is well known. Reservations are suggested.

Espuma

28 Wilmington Avenue
302-227-4199
www.espuma-restaurant.com

Espuma proudly claims that it is constantly re-creating itself. And regulars depend on that very thing for a memorable dining experience. Chef/owner and James Beard nominee Jay Caputo urges you to "Go ahead and lick the plate!" Do you really want to be seen doing that?

Espuma is quiet, dim and rather moody; lit by candles and sconces in warm crimson tones. Espuma's reputation for service is legendary: Efficient and exactly as friendly as it needs to be.

Go here if you're longing for foam, glaze and essence, or craving a new combination (sweet fennel ravioli, for example), or a new taste (pecorino fregola sarda, let's say). Caputo pushes the envelope and that's part of the fun. OK, make reservations, then go ahead and lick the plate.

Victoria's Restaurant in the Boardwalk Plaza Hotel

2 Olive Avenue
302-227-7169
www.boardwalkplaza.com/
victorias-restaurant

Victoria's is your best bet for waterfront fine dining in Rehoboth.

The entire hotel, from its bird-populated lobby to the multi-tiered china & crystal-filled dining room is reminiscent of a Victorian tea room (and, in fact, High Tea is offered by reservation).

In warm weather, opt for Boardwalk seating. Even on cool evenings, flaming columns of warmth cast a romantic glow over the boards and the sand.

Executive Chef Tom Deptula whips up fine breakfasts, lunches, dinners and a Sunday brunch accompanied by live piano music by the boardwalk. The lunch menu contains a variety of tasty and approachable surprises, including Victoria's famous crab melt. Ask about the Tuesday Veal & Vine specials.

Zebra

32 Lake Avenue
302-226-1160
www.ristorantezebra.us

Downscale, Zebra is not. Even on a humid evening, patrons are generally clad in long pants and collared shirts. When you make reservations, strive for a table on the wraparound front porch for an al fresco Lake Avenue.

The menu is user-friendly, with pasta plates and salad-based goodies on the left, and more elaborate meat/fish dishes on the right. The left side of the menu offers the pasta plates in half and whole portions. Do not miss the tortellini with peas and prosciutto in a rich, creamy sauce. Images of those little peas frolicking with crispy, thin-as-air prosciutto will haunt you.

$$$ MID-PRICED AND SOLID AS A ROCK:

Henlopen City Oyster House

50 Wilmington Avenue
302-260-9193
www.hcoysterhouse.com

Get there early for HCOH's raw bar happy hour, as servers elbow their way through the crowd with drinks, small plates and icy platters of raw oysters.

Seasoned owners Chris Bisaha and Joe Baker have sustained an enviable reputation for good service, as Chef Bill Clifton crafts remarkable dishes that belie the reasonable prices.

Little surprises abound, including fried oysters served North Carolina-style with chicken salad; creamy lobster mac & cheese and New England lobster rolls on the obligatory buttered, split-top roll.

Henlopen City Oyster House is open for lunch in the off-season. Do not miss the lobster reuben!

Salt Air

50 Wilmington Avenue
302-212-2409
www.saltairrestaurant.com

About 20 steps west of Henlopen City Oyster House is an equally delicious bargain: Salt Air. Owners Norm and Eric Sugrue wisely kept the "picnic" concept from the former owner, and memorable appetizers range from spiced nuts to crabby deviled eggs to oven-roasted chipotle/Old Bay wings.

Entrees vary, but some of the favorites from Chef Rebecca Krebs include fisherman's pot pie, Uncle Eric's bone-in pork chop, and shrimp & grits with chorizo. And don't miss the ground beef bolognese over pappardelle.

Pretty much anybody who is (or thinks they are) somebody can be found in the busy bar at least once a week. Get there early and score yourself a seat at the farm table strategically located in the shadow of Johnny Appleseed.

Confucius
57 Wilmington Avenue
302-227-3848
www.confuciusrehobothbeach.com
Shawn and Danielle Xiong have brought their beloved cuisine from Hunan Province to Rehoboth, and this tiny cottage is where Chinese food goes to learn how to be Chinese food.

Everything – everything – is prepared fresh to order, and must-haves include the cold spicy noodles, the Szechuan string beans, salt & pepper shrimp and calamari, whole crispy fish and hot pepper anything. If you are frightened by spicy food, don't worry: Simply tell your server and your dish will arrive fully flavored, but pepper-free. Confucius is happy to accommodate various and sundry food proclivities. Just ask.

Papa Grande's Rehoboth
210 Second Street
302-227-6494
www.papagrandes.com
This brand-new spot is a re-creation of the original Papa Grande's Coastal Taqueria in Fenwick Island. The 8th eatery on the Delaware coast opened by the late Matt Haley, Papa Grande dishes out popular Latino street food and indigenous favorites.

The chef adds little twists and turns, and suddenly a new world is there for the tasting: Goat, crispy fish, chicken and Spam & pineapple tacos are just part of the taco selection, and the lobster/corn quesadillas are already a legend. In short, it's Mexican and Latin American street-food kicked up a notch.

A value-added is the treehouse: Experience it at sundown with a big margarita.

Stoney Lonen
208 Second St.
302-227-2664
www.stoneylonen.com
It's all about Ireland at Bryan Lookup's dark and cozy eatery. In addition to a busy happy hour, Stoney Lonen offers a variety of tasty mains and appetizers, including the always delicious Guinness stout-braised short ribs, shepherd's pie made with deliciously seasoned lamb, smoked whiskey and fennel Irish bangers, and grilled brown bread.

Wash it all down with a pint or two. Cead Mile Failte!

Lupo di Mare in the Hotel Rehoboth
247 Rehoboth Avenue
302-226-2240
Another Matt Haley eatery, Lupo di Mare reflects his taste with austerity and clean lines. The menu stays with that theme with a minimum of heavy sauces or complex preparations. Lupo di Mare relies on the taste of high-quality ingredients to keep loyal guests coming back for more.

Do not miss the veal meatballs, the kale salad and the shrimp & sausage and grits. Top off your meal with some of the best tiramisu around.

Cultured Pearl
301 Rehoboth Avenue
302-227-8493
www.culturedpearl.us
Susan and Rob Wood's pan-Asian eatery is an institution in Rehoboth Beach. From the colorful sushi bar to the glass enclosed dining room to the extraordinary rooftop dining area (suspended over thousands of gallons of water teeming with colorful fish), the Cultured Pearl experience is a unique one.

Tempura preparations share the menu with Asian-inspired wings and steaming dumplings. And though sushi is certainly the main attraction, there's something for everyone on the large and diverse menu.

Make reservations if you want to enjoy the rooftop!

Stingray
59 Lake Avenue
302-227-6476
stingrayrestaurant.com
Stingray is the downstate gem in Cherry Tree Restaurant Group's triple crown of Delaware restaurants. The colorful sushi bar dominates the darkly elegant interior, glowing in shades of orange and red, – prime seating for those who love freshly crafted rolls and sashimi.

If you like the idea of sushi but prefer yours cooked, the Hairy Mexican is legendary not only at Stingray in Rehoboth, but also at its sister restaurant, Mikimoto's in Wilmington.. Sushi happy hour is the best deal in town, with 2-for-1 rolls. Top off your selections with a cold Sapporo.

Hobos
56 Baltimore Avenue
302-226-2226
www.myhobos.com
Chef Gretchen Hanson describes her cuisine as "global eco-fusion." Whatever that might mean, it ends up as tasty and unusually crafted dishes made with fresh and local ingredients. Though not primarily a vegetarian or vegan restaurant, Hobos is proud to cater to most any dining preference, and many of the vegan dishes are ordered by confirmed carnivores simply because they taste great.

Weekend seats at Hobos are a rare find, so always call for reservations.

JAM Bistro
21 Baltimore Avenue
302-226-5266
jambistro.com

JAM Bistro describes itself as "East of Eden," and that it is: Right next door to its sister restaurant, Eden (and a little closer to the Atlantic). JAM Bistro is as upbeat as Eden is sedate. Specials like homemade meatloaf, chicken and waffles and lamb shish kebab are not to be missed. JAM also has the distinction of being located in the same spot as one of Rehoboth's most beloved restaurants from the past, the Camel's Hump.

Enjoy outdoor and indoor dining on the ocean block. JAM is certainly the spot to see and be seen!

Lula Brazil
234 Rehoboth Avenue
302-212-2755
www.lulabrazil.com

Meg Hudson, former partner in Wilmington's Domaine Hudson, has brought the taste—and the sounds—of coastal Brazil to the old Cloud 9 location in Rehoboth Beach. Along with a spicy dance club, Meg and her talented crew are dishing up family-style dishes that suggest African and Mediterranean influences. Executive Chef Abde Dahrouch comes with impressive credentials that include Miami's La Terazza and Brasserie, along with Jean Pierre, La Brasserie, and Jean Louie in Washington, D.C. Opening late in the 2014 season, the early word was that Meg has brought her A-game to Lula Brazil.

Shorebreak Lodge
10 Wilmington Avenue
302-227-1007
shorebreaklodge.tumblr.com

Shorebreak Lodge is co-owned by the original owner and chef at Eden. Rob Stitt has teamed up with veteran bartender (and inveterate surfer) Matt Sprenkle to create a surfing-themed spot with quite a few surprises on the menu. Any soup with watermelon is to be ordered (Stitt works magic with this sort of thing), and upscale takes on down-home favorites like meatloaf and roast chicken are the order of the day.

Shorebreak Lodge is just steps from the Boardwalk and has a lively late-night bar scene.

$$ WALLET-FRIENDLY AND STILL A BARGAIN

Summer House
228 Rehoboth Avenue
302-227-3895

Summer House is known for its consistent, no-frills food. As one of Big Fish Restaurant Group's four Rehoboth eateries, a variety of steaks, big salads and mouthwatering appetizers (try the homemade chips with blue cheese!) are the order of the day.

Monday evening is Summer House's legendary burger night, with some special twists like the salmon burger only available on that night. Get there early! The burgers are a bargain at full price, so you can just imagine what happens when they are 50% off.

It's not all about Mondays, however, so watch for the Mooney's Iced Tea night and Steak Night.

Mariachi
14 Wilmington Avenue
302-227-0115

Owner Yolanda Pineda proclaims that "Mi casa es su casa!" And she means it. Her huge menu pays tribute to Salvadoran, Spanish and Mexican cultures, including handmade pupusas with spicy slaw and darkly sweet fried plantains. It is a rare moment that Ms. Pineda is not strolling from table to table making sure everything is all right. If the restaurant is not too busy, she is happy to go off-menu to create whatever your heart desires.

The upstairs dining room features a front porch with a view of the ocean. Weekend seats in the summer are few and far between, so it's always best to call first.

Semra's Mediterranean Grill
19 Rehoboth Avenue
302-381-5908
www.semras.com

This little spot on the ocean block looks like a beachy carryout, but behind that humble storefront lurks one of the best ethnic restaurants in Delaware. Semra Tekmen's Turkish cuisine is a direct result of her grandmother's influence, and Semra makes everything right there on the premises, including the Greek yogurt for her tangy tzatziki and the Middle Eastern hummus and babaghanouj.

Gyros on pita are sliced off of two slowly rotating vertical spits. Semra spices and builds her own gyro loaves and they couldn't be fresher. In the off-season, the restaurant features prix-fixe dinners that spotlight talented belly dancers.

Dos Locos

208 Rehoboth Avenue
302-227-3353
www.doslocos.com

If you're looking for Tex-Mex in Rehoboth Beach, Dos Locos is the place to go. All the standards are there, including burritos, tacos, quesadillas, rellenos and tamales. But there's more … The owners love to visit Mexico and bring back delicious recipes that feature fresh seafood, and entrees such as the shrimp and lobster burrito and the fish tacos are not to be missed.

Stonegrill dining is a value-added at Dos Locos, where you can cook your own dish on a 700 degree stone at your table. Needless to say, this is not recommended for kids, though the restaurant is very kid-friendly otherwise.

Enjoy the lively bar with multiple flavors of margaritas in three sizes, plus a long list of Mexican beers.

MIXX

26 Baltimore Avenue
302-226-8700
www.mixxrehoboth.com

Owner Ginger Breneman started out as a bartender in that very location long before it was MIXX. She is still behind the bar, and now she owns the place. MIXX is on the ocean block of Baltimore Avenue, directly across from JAM Bistro and Eden. Ginger never met an infusion she didn't like, and that results in some of the most delicious martinis in town.

Chef Dave Sauers keeps things basic but delicious, and Wednesday night burger and half-price martini nights are a tradition in Rehoboth Beach.

Zogg's

1 Wilmington Avenue
302-227-7660
www.zoggsbar.com

There's a little bit of Key West just a few steps from the Boardwalk, and it is Zogg's. Marked only by a blue awning, Zogg's is truly a hidden gem. But the search is worth it: crispy fried alligator, pulled pork sliders and some of the best rum cocktails await you at Zogg's. Half of the restaurant is outside under palm trees and colorful umbrellas. In the season, live steel drum music floats through the air as busy servers deliver nachos, specialty sandwiches and burgers (get the granny smith and brie burger!) to relaxed diners.

Fins Fish House & Raw Bar

243 Rehoboth Avenue
302-226-FINS
www.finsrawbar.com

When one thinks of Fins Fish House & Raw Bar, one must also think of Claws, its sister restaurant just a block east. It doesn't get much more beachy than these two long-standing Rehoboth restaurants. Fins is known for a huge selection of oysters and clams, along with a menu full of salads, spring rolls and mac & cheese recipes brimming with seafood. By the way, Fins' Bloody Marys are the stuff of Rehoboth Avenue legend.

Walk toward the ocean (and toward that hammering sound) and there is Claws, with brown-paper-covered tables brimming with steamed hardshell crabs and icy pitchers of beer. It's noisy, beachy and fun. Both restaurants are very busy in the summer.

Modern Mixture

62A Rehoboth Avenue
302-227-0600
www.modern-mixture.com

Another hidden gem marked only by a bright orange awning, Modern Mixture brings a much needed alternative to pizza, fries, and other takeout in the ocean block. Chef/owner Leo Cabrera fills the need for affordable, healthy, and delicious dine-in and takeout with a variety of Latin, Mediterranean, American and fusion plates.

Hearty burritos and tortas include beef, chicken breast, vegetarian, and pulled pork, and share the menu with healthy and delicious salads and smoothies.

Creative infused drinks include frozen red sangria. There's something for everyone at Modern Mixture.

Arena's

149 Rehoboth Avenue
302-227-1272
www.arenasdeliandbar.com

In Rehoboth Beach, the word "Arena's" is synonymous with "sandwiches." The sandwich menu is extensive, and you can even build your own. Heaping plates of nachos, stuffed tacos and shelf after shelf filled with craft beers round out the informal, noisy and fun atmosphere.

Specialties at Arena's include the mountainous BLT, the Philly cheesesteak, the chicken salad club and the Italian Stallion (yes, that is a sandwich!).

The Rehoboth Foodie is the author of Rehoboth In My Pocket: The indispensable travel guide to Rehoboth, Dewey and Lewes. With this app on your Apple or Android phone, you'll arrive as a visitor, but you'll live like a local!

THE BEACHFRONT PIZZA WARS

By The Rehoboth Foodie

I t's half-past dusk. The lights of Rehoboth Avenue cast a celebratory glow on the smiling, strolling humanity. The salty breeze triggers an odd feeling – an unexplained emptiness. It nags at you. What more could you possibly need on such an idyllic evening by the Atlantic? The answer is easy: A slice of pizza, of course!

Pizza is like barbecue and other regional foods: Everybody is convinced that their favorite is the best. And Rehoboth dishes up a variety of savory pies guaranteed to satisfy even the most demanding *pizzaphile*.

Oceans attract pizza. Wherever big waves break on sandy beaches, you can be sure that cheese is bubbling nearby. The sheer availability of the stuff makes it easy to pick and choose a favorite.

Lunch, owned by Nick Papantinas. Those of us *of a certain age* might remember the big "Have You Had Your Potatoes Today" sign, replete with the obligatory dancing potatoes. Louie Gouvas still keeps a close eye on operations when he's not riding his bike around town greeting his loyal followers.

LOUIE'S PIZZA
(11 Rehoboth Avenue, 302-227-6002)

Tim and Tony Gouvas have been running the Rehoboth Avenue icon since they could barely see over the counter. Louie's thin and yeasty crust has an appetizing "pull" that takes center stage without hogging the spotlight. The boys are well-known for pilin' on the pepperoni, and somehow their pizza tastes even better when a slice (or two … or four) is reheated and consumed while inspecting the surf from the Boardwalk.

Tim and Tony's dad opened Louie's in 1974 when the place was associated with another piece of Rehoboth history, George's

GROTTO
Main Rehoboth Location: 36 Rehoboth Avenue, 302-227-3278

NICOLA
Original Location: 8 N. First Street, 302-227-6211

The two Goliaths of Pie, have been crankin' 'em out for hungry vacationers since about the time

and the rest is turnover history. The classic Nick-O-Boli can be stuffed with pretty much anything that can top a pie, and Nicola Pizza has earned a loyal following. So, is it the hot and cheesy pizzas, or the half-moon shaped Nick-O-Bolis that elicit so much dedication? Must we choose? It really doesn't matter: Both locations of Nicola Pizza are jam-packed in the summer season, and the Caggianos have no plans to mess with success!

the ocean was installed. As they defiantly face-off on Rehoboth Avenue – Grotto to the south, Nicola to the north – each saucy empire enjoys an army of militant enthusiasts. So why are there two? Read on ….

It all started with Grotto. In 1960, Dominick Pulieri introduced a thin-crust pie that shares a distinctive trait with many Chicago deep-dish versions: The sauce is applied on top of the secret blend of cheeses. The delicate crunch when it's well-done lends credence to what Grotto proudly calls "that legendary taste." Another Pulieri trademark is the spiral design created when the sauce is swirled onto the pizzas from a handheld applicator.

When Dominick opened the very first Grotto Pizza on Rehoboth Avenue, nobody in this rural Delaware town had any idea what a "pizza" was. So he and his family stood out on the sidewalk, dispensing slices to raise beachgoers' collective consciousness about that newfangled, strangely addictive triangle. Now there are three separate locations in downtown Rehoboth where the craving for that legendary taste can be satisfied.

In 1971, Nick and Joan Caggiano opened Nicola Pizza. Nicola's crust is smooth and softer than Grotto, and their slightly sweeter sauce is topped with the cheese. Take a whole pizza, fold it over like a big hot turnover, and you have Nicola's signature Nic-O-Boli, a cross between a calzone and a stromboli. Forget the details. It's tasty, and was initially available only to Nick's employees.

But after a while it appeared on the menu,

CASA DiLEO
721 Rehoboth Avenue, 302-226-8660

The western reaches of Rehoboth Avenue host Casa DiLeio. Owner and chef John DiLeo's gigantic two-hander lunch slice is served thin and New York style. The whole pie is bigger than a Chrysler hubcap and several times as heavy. Pizza *cognoscenti* fold the slice lengthwise and consume it wood-chipper style with their favorite toppings. Originally the owner of Tutto Bene restaurant out on the highway, John now concentrates his efforts on the Rehoboth Avenue location and Casa DiLeo North, a relatively recent satellite location in the Midway Galleria Center.

Visit RehobothFoodie.com for honest, insightful reviews and commentary on Rehoboth Beach area restaurants. Contact at foodie@RehobothFoodie.com.

CONVERSATION: SAM CALAGIONE
Founder and President, Dogfish Head Craft Brewery

Sam Calagione and wife Mariah met at boarding school (Northfield Mount Hermon) in western Massachusetts, where he grew up (and spent summers in Dogfish Head, Maine). She was raised in Delaware. At 25, after having made "maybe a half-dozen batches of home-brew in my life," they launched the first brewery to open in Delaware since Prohibition in 1995 with the Dogfish Head Brewings & Eats in Rehoboth Beach ("I fell in love with the area and wanted to open a brewery in a state that didn't have one").

"We were following the first generation of craft brewers, Sam Adams and Sierra Nevada. They made all-natural, flavorful beers but they were still referencing the traditional European beer style based on grain and hops. I wanted to do the first brewery that looked at the entire culinary landscape for potential brewing ingredients like chicory and allspice and pumpkin meat and maple syrup (which still comes from my family's trees). That was our whole goal.

Exotic beer like that had to be 'hand sold' to get people to try them, so having a restaurant was part of the plan right from the start. It's hard to believe now, but in 1995 people called us crazy to try to stay open year-round that far from the highway and in the other direction from the boardwalk. They called our area of Rehoboth Avenue "No Man's Land" when we opened; there was no restaurant on our block.

For marketing, we printed up laminated cards and gave them to 25 local businesses to put at their cash registers, offering 25% discounts for the store owners who let us put them there and half-priced pints to customers who brought in the coupons. I'd ride around on my bike every week to re-stock them.

The kitchen was profitable from the very first year. The brewery, which was at Nassau Commons in Lewes from 1997 through 2001, lost money for three straight years. We had to shovel money in from the restaurant to keep it going. Nationally, we're known for beer but if it hadn't been for the restaurant, we would have gone bankrupt. It still represents about 7 percent of company revenue.

The Milton brewery is the heart and major distribution artery of Dogfish Head, but the Rehoboth pub is our soul—our point of origin and the karma that kept the brewery going in hard times.

At the front of our Rehoboth Brewpub, there have always been two neon signs: 'Wood-Grilled Food' and 'Home-Made Beer'. Those two things are the foundations of our company. That's what we set out to do and continue to do: pair rustic foods with rustic beer, and rustic beer with rustic food. I had read about the 'new' American food in the 1990s and what people like Alice Waters at Chez Panise in California were doing with local, native ingredients. I wanted us to be part of that natural food movement and the first in the country to take it in a beer-centric foodie direction.

One of the smartest things I did when I was 25 was include a clause in our lease for the Pub. I knew we were paying a high rent so, in return, the landlord Donna Stone agreed that if we were still in business five years later, we could buy the building with all that accrued back rent serving as credit for 20% of the appraised value of the real estate. Which we did. ∎

Dogfish Head Brewings & Eats
320 Rehoboth Avenue
302-226-2739

DOGFISH HEAD BREWERY: SOMETHING FOR EVERYONE.

Rain or shine, there's always a line at Dogfish Brewings & Eats on Rehoboth Avenue. But you can also experience another world of Dogfish cuisine at Sam Calagione's brewery in Milton.

The first impression you get when entering the Cannery Village development is how *big* the place is! A phalanx of fermentation tanks towers over the one-of-a-kind Steampunk Treehouse and two bocce ball courts. Suddenly it gets even better as you detect the aroma of grilling brats.

Follow the music into a huge indoor area surrounding a colorful bar and country-style farm tables. Once you get your bearings, step up to the counter. If you're lucky you'll place your order with the enthusiastic Dogfish head himself.

And the brats!

Like your brat hot? Get the Spicy Espresso version. Made with chicken, it's surprisingly light and gets a heady kick (and a whisper of licorice root) from Calagione's Chicory Stout.

I like to slather it with DFH's very grainy, very colorful and oh so spicy Thai mustard - and maybe a polite drizzle of Firefly Ale hot sauce for good measure.

If you're not feeling that adventurous, the basic pork Bratwurst is infused with the fruity Raison d'Extra. Or the Heirloom Italian, bringing with it the suggestion of chardonnay from DFH's Midas Touch. It pairs perfectly with cold and frothy Tweason'ale (brewed for those allergic to gluten, but enjoyed by all). Or the Greek Feta, another chicken version that shares the Midas Touch with the Italian. All the grilled goodies are happily enrobed in a soft and yeasty brewer's grain bun baked exclusively for Dogfish Head by Touch of Italy.

Be sure to try the Brooklyn Brine Hop-Pickles that are on the menu, made in a tiny Brooklyn picklery where bright green cucumbers are infused with Dogfish Head 60-Minute IPA. ■

by Bob Yesbek

DIVERSIONS
& Entertainment

REHOBOTH FLORAL HALLMARKS

"A heavy surf pounds the Delaware shore at Rehoboth Beach. To escape its insistent roll and splash, one may walk back into the cool, fragrant woods of oak and dogwood, pine and holly. Among the luxuriant growth of those indigenous trees, the roadsides and cottages are planted with a wealth of figs, mimosas, pyacanthas, crepe myrtles, privet and box among other imports."

Mary Louise Speed, 1948

Seldom are full canopies of deciduous forest seen so close to the shoreline, but the relatively high elevation of Rehoboth Beach and the Cape Henlopen region allow for uncommon variation in foliage. Proximity to the Atlantic Ocean means winter temperature is a few degrees warmer here than in most of Sussex County, enabling local gardeners to extend their range.

With so many summer residents in Rehoboth, much of the emphasis is on potted tropical and exotic annuals. According to Donna DeAngelis, co-owner of Tomato Sunshine— the family-run garden near Holland Glade Road —summer gardening is all about the blossom (after an up-front investment in classic perennials). With decades of providing at-home gardeners and landscapers with their greenery, she's learned no garden in the nation's summer capital is complete without these hallmark perennials and sensational bloomers.

CREPE MYRTLE

Crepe Myrtle, or Lagerstroemia, account for nearly 50 species of deciduous and evergreen trees and shrubs known primarily for two things: long-lasting flowers that bloom throughout the summer months; and the mottled appearance of trunks due to bark that sheds year-round. These days, crepe myrtles are available in a wide variety of colors and blooms that represent the quintessential Rehoboth beach cottage accessory.

HYDRANGEA

The classic look of Hydrangea blossoms are still ubiquitous to the Rehoboth Beach cottage landscape, but De'Angelis says these big blooms are tougher and more colorful than ever: "There is something with these varieties of Hydrangea that take the heat better and bloom all summer," she said. "This is different from our grandmother's hydrangea, which had the big pompom bloom once a summer and that was it.

KNOCKOUT ROSES

Since Knockout Roses were introduced in 2000, these low-maintenance blooms have become a standard accompaniment to many local gardens. With so many beach houses filled only seasonally, Rehoboth landscaping tends to be focused more on small beds and potted plants for pops of color, rather than native landscape. That's the perfect setting for Knockouts. With showy, continuous blooms in a compact habitat, these roses have become a low-maintenance solution for success.

MAY NIGHT SALVIA

Hardy, long-blooming May Night Salvia provides gardeners with densely-packed blossoms of lavender blue color from late May into August. Clustered at the circle on Rehoboth Avenue, this outdoor perennial provides a colorful greeting for visitors at the entry to town. When properly deadheaded, this perennial may also re-bloom in late summer.

DOGWOOD TREES

With their colorful blooms and compact size, Dogwood trees have long been beloved in Rehoboth Beach. Blooming in early spring, the Dogwood can grow from 15 to 25 feet, although typically more wide than tall. Often incorporated into landscaping as understory trees in semi-shaded areas or foundation plantings, Dogwoods may grow in a variety of soil types but require good drainage for their shallow root systems.

MANDEVILLA

For more exotic vines, the trumpet-shape blooms of Mandevilla flower in shades of pink, white or red. Flourishing in a pot or along a trellis, the lush, tropical vine is deer resistant and may grow to 20 feet. Typically grown as an annual, this poisonous vine blooms through the summer and fall.

AMERICAN HOLLY

Easily grown in average, well-drained soil, the Ilex Opaca, or American Holly tree, is another often seen accompaniment to the landscape of Rehoboth Beach. Most frequently found in moist woods, forest bottomlands and swamp peripheries plus some coastal dunes, the species is the only native U. S. holly with spiny green leaves and bright red berries. This is the Christmas holly whose berry-laden boughs are typically collected at Christmas time each year for ornamentation ("decking the halls"). Indeed, before the days of plastics, Sussex County was known as a winter holly-wreath making mecca, mailing wreaths nationally from the neighboring town of Milton, which celebrates this history with the holly festival each year in December.

MIMOSA

Technically considered an invasive species that reduces sunlight and nutrients for native plants, Mimosas are also known as silk trees. First imported to the United States from China in 1745 and cultivated through the 1800s primarily as an ornamental, their leaf arrangement gives the Mimosa a fern-like or feathery appearance. Mimosa flowering occurs from May through July, when globular flowers composed of individual stamen are borne in terminal clusters at the base of the current year's twigs. The flowers are fragrant and pink in color, about 1½ inches long. Mimosa reduces sunlight and nutrients available to desired species because of the denseness of the stand.

FIG TREES

Easy-to-grow Fig Trees have long been part of Rehoboth greenery as their shallow root systems adapt well to containers and almost all types of soil. With regular pruning, trees can be kept as small as 6 inches or as tall as 30 feet. The versatile fruit can be eaten fresh or used for cooking and baking. Chef Hari Cameron of a(Muse) restaurant on Baltimore Avenue, for example, usually keeps one on hand near his kitchen.

PYCANTHAS

Known for its mass of white flowers in summer, followed by orange-red berries in the autumn, thorny, evergreen Pycanthas are the large shrubs sometimes known as Firethorns. This hardy plant's bright-orange berries typically draw migrating birds through the fall and winter when food is scarce. Most often used as a large landscape shrub, Pycathas typically grow to 18 feet tall, and equally wide.

THE PARKS OF REHOBOTH

With the city being only one square mile, its several parks are relatively small in scale.

Coming into Rehoboth off Route 1 via Rehoboth Avenue, you will find Grove Park. It is located at the far western end of Rehoboth Avenue, immediately behind the Chamber of Commerce Visitor's Center. A weekly Farmer's Market occurs here on Tuesdays and is a great place to "buy local" and fresh. A beautifully landscaped area at the entrance was designed and planted by market volunteers with the help of city staff. There's a playground and two pavilions available for rent by contacting the city.

Cranberry Park is home to the Garden of the Navigators and located at the western end of Lake Gerar, bordered by Olive and Third Streets. Beautifully landscaped, it is a lovely area for reflection, taking your morning coffee or reading a book. This beautiful garden commemorates Rehoboth's relationship to its "Sister City" Greve in the Chianti region of Italy and was designed to mirror the more formal gardens found there. It honors Greve's most famous navigator, Giovanni Verrazano who explored the Atlantic Coast.

The focus of the garden is an inlaid compass rose, an old design element found on maps. The "rose" term derives from the fairly ornate figures used with early compasses to represent the eight principal winds comprising the four cardinal directions (N, E, S, W) plus the four "intercardinal" or "ordinal directions" (NE, SE, SW, NW), at angles of difference of 45°.

Also in Cranberry Park, you can find an area for tossing a football or Frisbee as well as some swings, a picnic table and benches overlooking Lake Gerar. This is a neighborhood park, albeit on a small scale.

Lake Gerar Tot Lot and park grounds are located off First Street along Lake Avenue. It contains a substantial playground in the area behind the Henlopen Hotel/Condos at the north end of the boardwalk. The park grounds border Lake Gerar and offer tree-lined paths for strolling, dog walking, and benches for appreciating the lake. The water's edge is maintained in a natural habitat with native plantings and blooming colors in every season— a perfect place to enjoy the serenity of Lake Gerar.

Mariner's Park is another passive area adjacent to the Henlopen Hotel/Condos. Triangle-shaped and small, it offers a natural habitat reminiscent of the dunes. ∎

CONVERSATION: RAY ZEBROWSKI
Landscape Architect, Garden of the Navigators

Ray Zebrowski, a landscape architect licensed in six states, has been coming to Rehoboth since 2000. "I don't have a distinct style in my work," he says, preferring instead to use a wide variety of design from formal to naturalistic.

"The Garden of the Navigators project originated in 2012, when Pat Coluzzi, President of the Rehoboth Beach Sister City Association, asked me to collaborate on a garden in Greve in Chianti, our Italian 'sister'. The relationship between Greve and Rehoboth had its roots in 2008 when Rehoboth erected a monument honoring Greve native Giovanni da Verrazano, who mapped mapped the Cape region during a 1524 voyage along the Atlantic coast.

We designed the Italian garden with elements that reflected Rehoboth Beach: a white picket fence, lots of white benches, gravel, brick paths done in a herring-bone pattern like the hardscape on Rehoboth Avenue. Much of the incorporated plant material was also local with Crepe Myrtle and Knockout roses, ornamental grasses, day lilies, and azaleas. The Italians just loved it; they had a parade for the opening with some 200 local people.

The same year, we began planning a park here to honor our Italian sister city. The design went through many revisions. The original concept encompassed all 16,000 square feet of Cranberry Park with the focal piece in the center and paths that took you down to the lake's edge where there would be a children's playground. There was much public sentiment, though, to leave it as open space and grass.

I went back to the drafting table four or five times for revision. We finally got to a point where we could salvage much of the concept within a 5,000 square foot area. This is what you see today.

The compass is symbolic of the explorers Verrazano and Vespucci who first charted this coast using a compass. The design in the paving pattern is very Italianesque; I used a combination of pavers that were like a detailed, ornate rug. There are pinpoint lights in the pavers that reflect the stars, they are strategically placed to help 'navigate' visitors through the park in the evening.

The plantings have an Italian feeling. I used lavender, although it is somewhat temperamental at the beach. We incorporated Jerusalem sage and rosemary. The irises were brought over from Italy and given to us by the Mayor of Greve; they are very light blue in color, something that is very prominent in Tuscany area.

The Garden of the Navigators is for the residents and visitors alike. I want everybody to experience and understand the importance of the sister cities and say 'hey, the explorers of the Delaware coastline in the 1500s are still part of our history'." ∎

Garden of the Navigators
3rd Street and Lake Avenue

CLEAR SPACE THEATER

The Clear Space Theater Company is a resounding success story since its' inception in 2004, raising the standard of 'community theater' with unexpectedly high levels of professionalism when it comes to staging, acting, and singing-and-dancing.

Clear Space mounts productions in a wide variety of theatrical styles. The year-round season typically includes three popular Broadway shows, two musicals, two dramatic plays, a children's play, and the annual tradition of The Christmas Carol presented as an original musical. The resident acting company offers well over one hundred performances a year (and draws in excess of 20,000 patrons).

The company has evolved into a showcase, housed in a 335-seat theater at 20 Baltimore Street. In addition, the company supports an Arts Institute, which each year trains some 700 students in after-school and summer programs.

There are also full semester acting classes for adults and private coaching for auditions. Statewide community outreach is accomplished through the Company's partnership with The Schwartz Center for the Arts in Dover and the Freeman Stage in Fenwick Island. In addition, the Encore Thrift Shop, raises money through the sale of donated clothing. ∎

CONVERSATION: DOUG YETTER
Clear Space Theater Artistic Director, Co-Founder

Clear Space Theater marks its tenth anniversary in 2014, bringing to Rehoboth professional theater of a stature most unlikely in a small beach town. Doug Yetter, Artistic Director and Co-Founder, is a long-time veteran of musical theater, having served as a director, conductor, and composer of hundreds of productions.

"Rehoboth Beach had been a regular vacation spot for me prior to leaving Manhattan and moving here in 2004. At the time I commented (with some frequency) that a great summer theatre was needed. When we got here, it was clear that the gap had to be filled. It took several years to attract the talent that was already here and provide continuing training, but the amazing part of the company is that only a small percentage of the talent is imported. Almost everyone is local.

The name 'Clear Space' refers directly to our aesthetic. I like to dive right into the roots of a great show, and can't abide the 'smoke and mirrors' used to disguise weak shows. Consequently, rather than create full sets, we strive for a 'clear space' where the acting is preeminent, with great costumes and lights as support. Just a nightstand and part of a bed, for example, might represent a full bedroom. I much prefer having the audience let their imaginations fill in any blanks.

The theatre is three-quarter round plus a proscenium stage, so no audience member is ever more than five rows from the stage (with only three rows on the sides). There's truly not a bad seat in the house.

Our season is in alignment with the calendar and I plan two and three years in advance. We've gotten into a fairly regular groove: comedy in February; classic musical in March and April; newer, edgy musical in May. Summer Rep includes a family musical, more 'adult' musical, and several plays. We do a holiday show in December and also offer spring

and fall productions from our Broadway Bound Youth Theatre.

Our summer season is laid out so that you can see all three shows in one week, or on subsequent weekends. ∎

REHOBOTH JAZZ FESTIVAL

Unlikely as it may seem, Rehoboth Beach becomes one of the hot spots on the national music scene for a packed four days in October when it hosts the annual Rehoboth Jazz Festival, 25 years old in 2014.

While its registered trademark as 'the greatest jazz festival in the world' might be a slight stretch, the event has grown from its start on a single stage to something of a pilgrimage. "As I travel around the country," says organizer Dennis Santangini, "as far away as Napa Valley, California and Atlanta, people have heard about our festival."

Performers from past seasons have included national musicians and Grammy winners such as BB King, Dionne Warwick, Queen Latifah, Bob James, Foreplay, and Pacquito D'Rivera and, in 2014, Al Jerreau.

A big reason such big names come to the Rehoboth Beach Jazz Festival is because of the rare intimacy of the stages and opportunity to interact with audiences. With sites in Rehoboth Beach, Dewey Beach, and Lewes, the sounds of jazz and the spirit of celebration take over the area in a non-stop schedule of concerts and gigs.

The Festival is presented by the not-for-profit Delaware Celebration of Jazz. ∎

www.rehobothjazz.com

CONVERSATION: DENNIS SANTANGINI
Director of Rehoboth Jazz Festival

A Philadelphia native, Dennis Santangini started coming to Rehoboth Beach in the late 1970s, and loved it so much that he sold his gas station in Pennsylvania to move down full-time. He built and operated the Sea Witch Manor bed-and-breakfast on Lake Avenue. Following the death of his wife, during which time "the community was right there for me," Dennis was asked to take over the Rehoboth Jazz Festival in 1996. "It was my way of paying back."

"I'm not a musician but I've been a music lover all my life. My whole family was in show business. My cousin Pamela Stanley sings at the Blue Moon, she was the 'disco queen' of Europe comparable to Donna Summer in America. My father was an opera singer. I can't even sing in the shower, I just have a business mind.

When I became Director, the Festival had been going for five years, since 1991. Many people in the business community saw this as a great way to bring a 'second season' to Rehoboth but they couldn't devote full time to it. There were rock festivals and country festivals around the country but not many jazz festivals even though jazz was very popular at the time.

The Festival has changed through the years. It's not true 'straight-ahead' jazz anymore; it's closer to R&B and soft rock. There's more melody to the music now,' it's 'smooth jazz' because it has flair and gets people jumping up-and-down rather than just sitting there listening.

I'm responsible for booking the acts. I like the new style jazz. The old style jazz was born during the late-thirties and early-forties, the musicians who created it are dying off and the music is starting to fade out. There aren't many new artists in straight-ahead jazz. Maybe it will have a strong comeback someday. We work well over a year in advance. I look up who is selling tickets and who's not, who's travelling around and where, who will play with whom as openers.

Artists like playing Rehoboth, especially since we registered our trademark as 'The Greatest Jazz Festival in the World' several years ago. We get big names: B.B. King, Al Jarreau, Boney James, Sheila E, Queen Latifa, Dionne Warwick, Dave Kos and so many more.

The biggest venue is the performing arts center at Cape Henlopen High with 865 seats. It's an absolutely fabulous room. There are no bad sight lines and the building was built for sound. There are side panels in the ceiling that absorb different sound frequencies so the acoustics are perfect. Performers are blown away.

Our other big venue is the Rehoboth Beach Convention Center. It's not tiered theater seating but a big open hall. After Queen Latifah performed there, she gave me a big hug and said 'it's so intimate in Rehoboth, I love it.' I asked her 'why don't you stay with Hollywood, where you make so much money?' She looked out at the scene and said 'yeah, but this is fun!'

The toughest thing about operating the Festival is getting community support. We are now bringing about 15-thousand people into town for the Festival to buy gas, book hotels, eat food, and shop. But we don't get much back. Producing the festival costs well over $100,000 for things like lights, sound, insurance, renting vehicles, hotel rooms and food. That's before any artist fees.

We're non-profit. Every year we make a contribution to the Beebe Medical Foundation and small non-profit organizations. We need the business community to buy tickets even if they end up giving them away to make sure we sell out.

For me, the most fun is standing at the back of the room watching the people's faces and asking them how they enjoyed the show. The answer is always 'Oh my God, it was great, it was unbelievable.' It's so fulfilling, it gives you chills." ∎

REHOBOTH FILM SOCIETY

The Rehoboth Beach Film Society started in 1997 when five local citizens, eager to bring more varied cinema to the area, invited the public to a screening in a local restaurant.

From those modest beginnings has evolved the celebrated Rehoboth Beach Independent Film Festival, a premiere cultural event. The five-day Festival in November showcases approximately 100 independent American and international films including features, documentaries, and shorts along with seminars and special events.

"I have real respect for the art of film," says Executive Director Sue Early, who originally came to Rehoboth Beach in 1998 to open a restaurant. "It is a great form of communication to increase people's awareness."

In addition to the Film Festival, the Society offers a year-round schedule of programs. "Delmarva Roots" is a winter series shown in conjunction with the Milton Historical Society, highlighting local filmmakers and local subjects (such as artist Howard Pyle, or the Delaware oyster industry). There is another series called "What Makes Us Tick", films followed by conversation led by mental health professionals; past themes have been "Families Taking the Gloves Off from Conflict to Understanding," and "Portraits of Intimacy: Exploring Family, Friendship, Love and Betrayal."

In addition, during the summer season the Society screens monthly family-oriented 'cinema by the surf' outdoors at the Rehoboth Beach Beachstand (and Canalfront Park in Lewes).

After 2014, the Film Society will be organizing new screening sites for the Festival after years at the Midway Theaters and the convenience of 'park and stay the day' at one location. "The Festival will take on a different flavor," says Sue Early. "We're looking at schools and churches. We may spread it out longer. Our goal is to build our own venue." ∎

www.rehobothfilm.com

courtesy of Portraits In the Sand

COASTAL CONCERTS

Coastal Concerts has been bringing classical music worthy of a metropolitan center to the area for more than a decade. It was founded to promote the appreciation of classical music in central Delmarva through multiple concerts every year.

Accomplished artists from around the world have played here (usually at the Bethel United Methodist Church Hall in Lewes at 4th and Market Street), including the internationally recognized pianist Misha Dichter. Other celebrated performers have included the Israeli Chamber Project, Spanish Brass Quintet, Chicago String Quartet, Lincoln Trio, and Chinese pianist Di Wu.

In addition to producing performances, since 2006 Coastal Concerts has awarded nearly $20,000 in scholarships to local high school students to help them continue their musical education. These awards are part of a comprehensive education and outreach campaign that also includes free public concerts, donation of used but playable musical instruments to local schools, and classroom visits by selected artists.

In conjunction with its outreach, Coastal Concerts also offers free admission to its regularly scheduled programs to young people ages 10 to 18 with one accompanying adult, and makes discounted tickets available to students 19 and older with a valid school ID. ∎

www.coastalconcerts.org

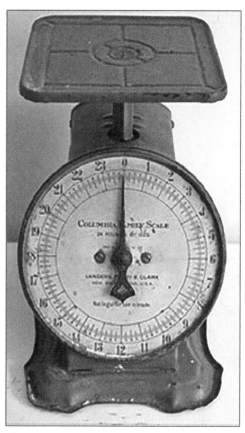

Photos are a range of antique objects that have been offered at local auction and sale.

ANTIQUING

CONVERSATION: THOMAS DE PRINCE

New Jersey native Thomas De Prince got hooked early in life on collecting, "anything and everything" from paper weights to bronze to art glass to furniture to paintings. A Ph.D. child psychologist by professionhis passion for objects would become a full-time pursuit.

Forty-two years ago he passed through Rehoboth Beach en route back from a show in North Carolina, fell in love with the town, and moved here. Although no longer in the commercial trade, his ardor remains undiminished. His home has been re-modeled and expanded

five times to house a mind-boggling array of museum-quality work ("if I like it, I find a place for it").

"Antiquing is like treasure hunting, that's what it's all about. Delaware is a fabulous place to do it because there's no sales tax. Dealers and sellers don't have to worry about tax identification numbers and collecting taxes for the state. It's so easy to do business here. It's not the same anywhere else in the trade, elsewhere dealers need a different tax ID for each location. That's why they love to show in Delaware, because it's so easy.

There are two general sorts of 'local specialties' to look for around Rehoboth. One is what you might call 'artisan' furniture and objects that were made by Delaware-area craftsmen of high quality with a sense of style and aesthetics. The other category is 'cottage,' objects that come from the grand old summer homes that were built around Rehoboth by the likes of the DuPonts and their friends. Typically the houses become too big and expensive to maintain, the kids liquidate the contents and all kinds of things from elegantly sculpted fireplace mantles to silver salt-and-pepper shakers show up for sale.

The Rehoboth area is very, very good for antiquing. The Annual Delaware Coast Antiques Show (usually in early September) at the Rehoboth Convention Center is very high end with dealers from all over the country featuring 18th and 19th century primitive and period furniture, early china and glassware, kitchen and fireplace accessories, export porcelain, and fine jewelry.

The Merchant's Attic at the Convention Center in early spring can be a good source for unlikely finds. It started out as a way for merchants to dispose of prior season's over-stock but has since blossomed into the state's 'largest garage sale.'

There is an annual Lewes Antiques Show and Sale at Bethel Methodist Church in Lewes (129 Fourth Street) that is particularly good for country objects. There's also an annual show on the grounds of the Lewes Historical Society. The antique mall on Second Street, Lewes Mercantile Antiques, always makes for an interesting visit that can sometimes prove rewarding." ∎

FISHING

Rehobeth is a lovely resort town, indeed, but is also an excellent place to take a fishing vacation.

Surf fishing is the main attraction for fisherman visiting the area. The town also offers great fishing opportunities in its back bay, as well as the Lewes and Rehoboth Canal. For those who want to cast for bigger sport, charter and head boat fishing is close by in Lewes and Dewey.

Surf fishing is excellent in Rehoboth from May to November. Striped bass show up in the surf mid-May, they are the main attraction for spring fisherman. Summer is a mixed bag of spot, sea trout, king fish, bluefish, flounder, dogfish, and skate rays. Fall brings the stripers back, mid-October thru November.

Some favorite surf fishing spots are the south side of the rock pile in front of the Henlopen Hotel, Tower Road, and 3R's Road. North of Indian River Inlet and the navy jetty in Cape Henlopen State Park are also choice venues. But just about any piece of beach bunker.

Good baits for the surf are cut bunker (menhaden) and clams for the big stripers of spring and fall. Baits for the summer are cut bunker, squid, shiners and bloodworms. Rigs to use are fish finder rig, top and bottom rig and the standard bottom rig. Hook and sinker size vary according to the species you're after and the roughness of the surf.

Rehoboth Bay is a Flounder fishing hot spot, as well as being full of spot and croaker all summer long. Of late have been reports of red drum in late summer. Rehoboth Bay is also an excellent place to take the family crabbing. Good baits for Rehoboth Bay are live minnows, squid and mullet for flounder fished on a flounder rig or fish finder. Baits for spot and croaker are bloodworms, squid, fish bites and night crawlers fished on top and bottom rigs or standard bottom rigs.

The Lewes-Rehoboth Canal on the backside of town is a great place to catch small stripers, flounder, and spot May thru October. The same baits and rigs used for the bay work equally well in the canal. It's also great for crabbing (chicken necks, salted eel and bunker make good bait).

From Rehoboth's beaches and bay to the canal, the fish are biting! ■

by Howard Hundley

BLUE FISH

Bluefish often appear off the coast in enormous numbers by June. Peak spawning season occurs in July (females can produce from nine hundred thousand to 4.5 million eggs), after which smaller fish enter the Chesapeake and Delaware Bays (larger large bluefish migrate north).

In general, bluefish are not hard to catch; they readily attack metal jigs and lures and take almost any cut or live bait. The high fat content of their dark meat makes it an 'acquired taste' for some but renders it excellent for smoking.

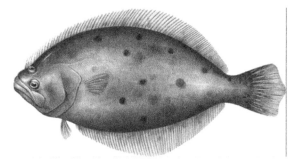

SUMMER FLOUNDER

Summer flounder spawn in the ocean, then move into the estuaries to grow for the next two years. Afterwards, they join the coastal spawning stock and spend the winter along the Continental Shelf to return in the spring to inshore coastal waters and bays.

Delmarva fishing pros know that flounders, as site feeders, don't bite much in dirty water. They need to see the bait! A key to being a good flounder fisherman is to find the cleanest possible water.

EXPLORATIONS

BURTON ISLAND TRAIL:
Delaware Seashore State Park, North end of Indian River Marina

This is an easy 1.6-mile round-trip walk along an elevated boardwalk through upland forests of oak, sassafras, holly and loblaly pine to the island that is an important nesting ground for the Diamondback Terrapin. There are grand vistas across the salt marsh to Indian River Bay and Rehoboth Bay. A wide variety of wildflowers abound. The trail is recommended during the cooler months of the year (since steamy summer heat is likely to make for a buggy experience).

HOLT'S LANDING STATE PARK SEAHAWK TRAIL
Route 26 between Bethany Beach and Dagsboro, on the south shore of Indian River Bay at the far end of the parking lot

This 1.7-mile loop is ideal for birders (the surroundings are populated with big birds like osprey, herons, hawks as well as songbirds). Wooded trails through bogs and marsh grass offer stunning views of Rehoboth Bay. This is a great place for young kids to fish and crab. The area was home to the native Nanticoke.

SAVAGES DITCH
Route 1, 6.6 miles south of Rehoboth Beach (Savage's Ditch Road) Delaware Seashore State Park

This is an ideal kayak launch spot for an area of Rehoboth Bay that is dotted with islands of coastal salt marsh that are favored nesting areas for native birds as well as exotics like Little or Common Black-headed gulls. Jetty rocks host Purple Sandpipers. There are Brown Pelicans in the warmer months.

THE GREAT CYPRESS SWAMP
Pocomoke River State Park
3461 Worcester Hwy, Snow Hill, MD 21863
(410) 632-2566

An hour's drive from Rehoboth 30 miles) straddling the Delaware-Maryland border, lies the Great Cypress Swamp whose waters ultimately feed into Rehoboth Bay. Its sand ridges and shallow depressions, some 50 square miles, are pre-Ice Age remains from when the Delmarva Peninsula was a desert of windblown dunes.

Fed by the Pocomoke River ("black water" in the indigenous language, the deep rich color created from the tannic acid in decaying cypress needles), this is the last place in Sussex County with remaining stands of the once abundant towering cypress trees that routinely grow 120 feet tall. The species, native to North America, dates back 300 million years. Cypress boards produced the shingles and siding of 18th century houses as well as wood for ship-building. Accounts from the time described trees eight and ten feet in diameter, standing so thick that "semidarkness prevailed beneath the canopy of their matted crowns."

During the Civil War, the swamp was an important link in the Underground Railroad, a landmark that fleeing slaves followed into Delaware and then safety in Pennsylvania.

It is home to 73 different breeding species of birds, ranging from the most common Worm-eating Warbler to the more rare Black-throated Green Warbler.

A self-guided two mile kayaking and canoeing paddle through the swamp can be launched from Pocomoke River State Park on the Maryland side.

Burton Island Trail

Holt's Landing

Savage's Ditch

Great Cypress Swamp

Willet

BIRDING

Rehoboth Beach and the surrounding area offer outstanding shore birding.

The action starts in late April through early June, as impressive numbers and diversity of sandpipers, plovers and others migrate through the region to freshwater impoundments and bay coasts. The fall migration begins in July, peaks in August and extends well into October. Species diversity in autumn is even better than spring, birder Life List trophies like Curlew Sandpiper and Ruff are relatively frequent.

From October through the end of the year, there are amazing concentrations of geese and fresh water duck species. "Watching tens of thousands of sparkling white Snow Geese spilling from a darkening blue sky into the marshes near Bombay Hook's Shearness Pool, the whole scene bathed in glowing, golden-orange by the low autumn sun, is a sight not soon forgotten," recounts one witness

During this same phase of late fall/early winter, the inland bays are populated with brant, goldeneye, common loons, horned grebes, buffleheads, and red-breasted mergansers. ∎

BIRDING SITES

Silver Lake offers what one birder calls "thrillingly close looks" at a variety of wintering duck species, especially Canvasbacks. It is also the most reliable place in the state to find Redheads, one or two of which can often be picked out from the hundreds of Canvasbacks, Ruddy Ducks and Mallards. Lesser and Greater Scaup also occur, along with a variety of gulls and other water birds.

Gordons Pond is prime spotting territory for the spring and fall arrivals of migrant songbirds, shorebirds, and raptors. In winter, flocks of Snow Geese and other waterfowl reside here (and are periodically spooked by the resident Bald Eagles). Northern Gannets, loons, and scoters can be seen flying over the ocean, located just 250 yards east. Summer features breeding Pine Warblers, Seaside Sparrows, and a few pairs of Piping Plovers. Throughout the year, the pine forest harbors roving bands of Brown-headed Nuthatches.

FAMILY FUN

Basketball Courts:
Rehoboth Elementary located on State Road, Rehoboth; John Waples Memorial Lions Club Park in Dewey Beach.
An indoor court is at the Sussex County Family YMCA in downtown Rehoboth.

Bicycling:
Sussex Cyclists (a local cycling group) leads day and evening rides from 11-50 miles mostly through rural Sussex County roads. Information is available at www.sussexcyclists.org or by calling the ride leader at 302-945-3360.

Boat Rides & Rentals
Join Lighthouse Pete the Pirate on a family-fun round trip cruise aboard the Cape May-Lewes Ferry every Sunday in July and August, 6:15pm departure. Info: www.cmlf.com or call 800-64-FERRY.

The Rehoboth Bay Marina in Dewey Beach is the place to go for boat rentals (as well as slips). Pontoon boats and runabouts are available for half or whole days, jet skis by the hour. Fishing poles, clam rakes, and crab lines can also be rented.
Rehoboth Bay Marina
109 Collins Ave.
Dewey Beach, DE 19971
(302) 226-2012
www.rehobothbaymarina.com

Take a sightseeing cruise or a sunset cruise from Fisherman's Wharf in Lewes or go on a dolphin/whale watch. 302-645-8862.

DiscoverSea Shipwreck Museum:
(708 Ocean Highway, Fenwick Island)

One of the largest collections of shipwreck and recovered artifacts in the Mid-Atlantic, complete with hands-on experience. Open daily June through August (11 am-8pm), Saturdays and Sundays the rest of the year (11am through 4pm) www.discoversea.com.

Golf:
Baywood Greens (Off Route 24, 32267 Clubhouse Way, Long Neck, DE (30 minutes from Rehoboth Beach), 302-947-9800
Beautifully landscaped ("like playing in a botanical garden") and maintained, 18 hole course that is "demanding but fair."

Rookery South Golf Club (27052 Broadkill Road, Milton DE 19968, (302)684-3000. Wide fairways, water features, doglegs and nature. "Challenging but fun" for all skill levels.

Kayaking
Kayaking at Cape Henlopen State Park (302)645-8983

Canoe and kayak rentals and excursions provided by Delaware State Parks. Sunset Kayaking Tour on the Bay paddles out to the Breakwater one night a week, reserve early (minimum age: 13). Eco kayak tours three mornings a week (minimum age: 8).

Tennis

Tennis courts can be found at the Rehoboth City Courts (302-227-3598) on Surf Avenue between Rehoboth Beach and North Shores; also at the Rehoboth Bay Sailing Association (302-227-9008).

In neighboring Lewes at Cape Henlopen High School, Canalfront Park in Lewes, and The Plantations in Lewes (call 302-526-5111 for info).

Fees may apply at some locations.

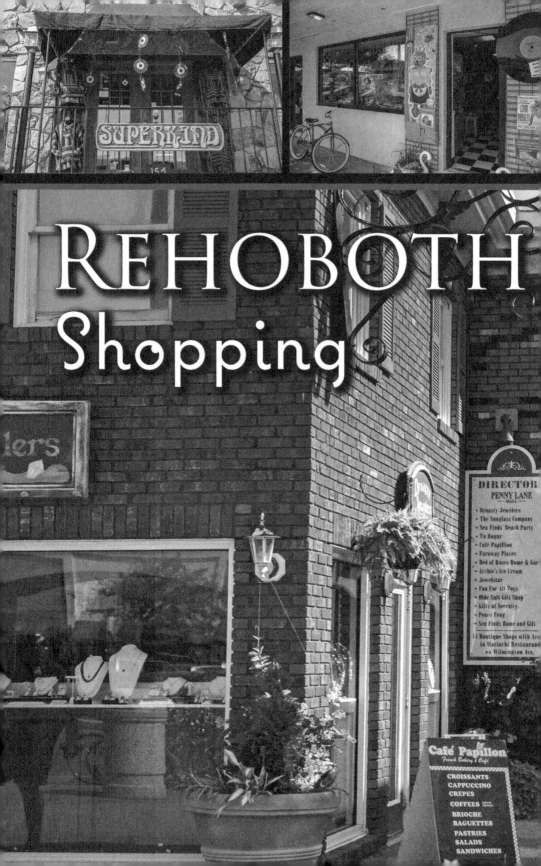

REHOBOTH
Shopping

DIRECTOR
PENNY LANE
— MALL —

- Dynasty Jewelers
- The Sunglass Company
- Sea Finds Beach Party
- Tu Hogar
- Café Papillon
- Faraway Places
- Bed of Roses Home & Gar
- Archie's Ice Cream
- Jewelstar
- Fun For All Toys
- Olde Salt Gift Shop
- Gifts of Serenity
- Peace Frog
- Sea Finds Home and Gift

14 Boutique Shops with Acc
to Mariachi Restaurant
on Wilmington Ave.

Café Papillon
French Bakery & Café

CROISSANTS
CAPPUCCINO
CREPES
COFFEES
BRIOCHE
BAGUETTES
PASTRIES
SALADS
SANDWICHES

SUPERKIND

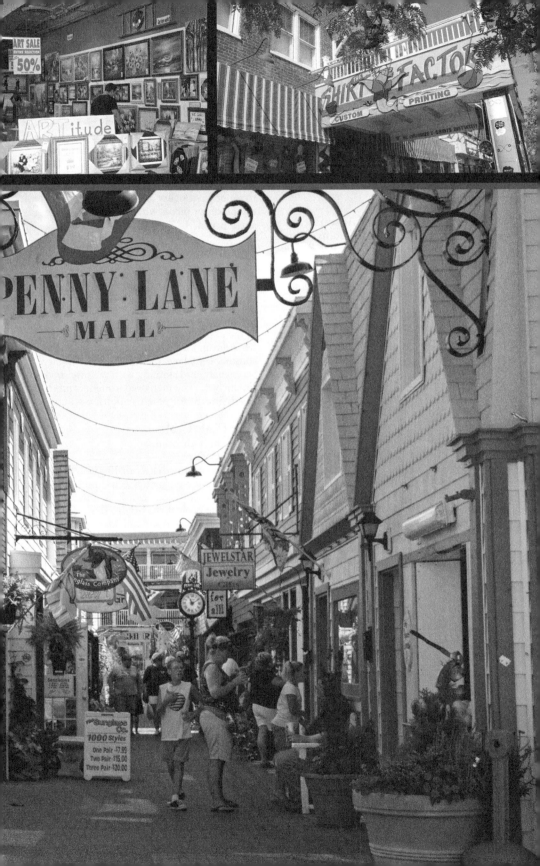

A SHOPPER'S GUIDE TO REHOBOTH BEACH

ALL THAT SHIMMERS: GEMSTONES AND FINE JEWELRY

Atlantic Jewelry
313 South Boardwalk
302-231-1678
Since Harry Keswani opened Atlantic Jewelry in 1987, he has not only managed to expand the business twice to become the largest fine jewelry store in the region at nearly 1,500 square feet but he has also gone on launch his own line of Harry K. custom jewelry.

Elegant Slumming
33 Baltimore Avenue
302-227-5551
Owner Frank Livingston opened Elegant Slumming in 1995 with a focus on fine jewelry, which has since broadened to add 'one-of-a-kind' decorative housewares including furniture, mirrors, and lamps.

Dynasty Jewelers
42 Rehoboth Avenue
302-227-1016
A prime choice for glitter, sparkle, and bling.

Stuart Kingston
One Grenoble Place (At the north end of the Boardwalk, adjacent to the Henlopen Hotel)
302-227-2524
A family-run business founded in 1930 as an auction house, Stuart Kingston has since added a retail facility to complement its year-round roster of estate auctions in such categories as silver, rugs and carpets, and collectibles. Jewelry is a specialty, including vintage and contemporary.

OUT AND ABOUT: APPAREL

Azura
139 Rehoboth Avenue
302-226-9650
Azura owner Alyssa Titus sells original designs and brings in brands that keep her stock of women's accessories, dresses, shoes, tops and bottoms looking modern, edgy and of-the-moment.

Downtown Cowgirl
146 Rehoboth Avenue
302-227-1917
This funky store carries a unique stock of affordable women's attire and accessories with tones of personality and originality. This is the place for pieces with 'big attitudes and small prices.'

Josephine's Daughter
146 Rehoboth Avenue
302-260-9577
Recently relocated to Rehoboth Avenue from a smaller location on Baltimore Avenue, Josephine's Daughter sells "wearable art" such as the popular graphic rain boots that make her store an ideal destination to prepare for the summer sun-shower. One-of-a-kind jewelry, accessories, and clothing with whimsy stock the shelves. The men's department is pretty much limited to game-fish bottle openers!

The Pink Crab
235 Rehoboth Avenue
302-260-9739
If you can't immediately distinguish the white cottage with a picket fence and pink shutters on Rehoboth Avenue as a Lilly Pulitzer boutique, one peek at the bright, floral pink and green prints inside will quickly confirm this signature store's position as the Rehoboth residence of the late 'Queen of Prep.'

Simply Dressed
33 Baltimore Avenue
302-227-2818
Simply Dressed is an upscale ladies boutique that retains the feel of an old beach cottage. The shopping experience here is comfortable, relaxed and friendly. Since its 2014 arrival in Rehoboth, the boutique has already proven itself a staple with simple elegance and premium service.

Sole
110 Rehoboth Avenue
302-227-3036
This contemporary women's boutique offers designer brands and classic styles with purses, shoes and a sale section with good finds. With a solid selection of kids clothing and

toys for the littlest vacationers at Sole Kids in the next retail unit, this women's boutique makes it tempting to let dad manage the tribe and sneak in for a quick shopping trip next door.

South Moon Under
118 Rehoboth Avenue
302-227-3806
When South Moon Under arrived in Rehoboth during the 90's, it was a small store with great finds but no method to its madness. Oh, how things change. These days, the upscale clothing and accessories store is the best place to get a chic, up-fashion pair of jeans. The store, like the clothes, looks like a million bucks.

Spahr
43 Baltimore Ave
302-226-3804
Designer Scott Spahr has been offering his hand-crafted men's and women's wear (manufactured in the shop) since 2000. There are also home décor products (think candles and pillows) and jewelry. Clean lines and crisp colors maintain this store's cool appearance, even as the summer heat melts most everything else.

EYE CANDY: GALLERIES AND STUDIOS

Gallery 50
50 Wilmington Ave.
302-227-2050
A contemporary art gallery, Gallery 50 is committed to featuring the works of Mid-Atlantic artists and promoting emerging artists as well. Exhibits tend to focus on the works of single artist, but Gallery 50 also hosts book signings, poetry readings and film screenings. With the more recent addition of a frame shop, Gallery 50 has become a full-service stop for art aficionados.

Heidi Lowe Jewelry Studio
328 Rehoboth Avenue
302-227-9203
Heidi Lowe is a jewelry designer who grew up on the Delaware seashore, a local girl. Hosting exhibitions of her own work and an array of international designers, her gallery is located in a cozy yellow beach cottage next to Dogfish Head brewpub. Here she works: creating new pieces, teaching classes, holding shows and celebrating the innovation of art jewelry design.

Kevin Fleming Gallery
239 Rehoboth Ave.
The celebrated local wildlife photographer and former National Geographic photo-journalist Kevin Fleming has opened his own shoebox-sized gallery on Rehoboth Avenue to showcase his work. Here, his gallery is stocked with breathtaking shots of coastal Delaware on paper (and canvas) as well as stunning coffee table books.

Ocean Gallery
26 Wilmington Ave.
302-225-9507
This venerable (five decades old) fine art gallery snakes its way through three buildings, from a weathered beach house on Wilmington Avenue where wall art overtakes even the porch. The maze leads through different rooms filled with oil paintings or photography and even trails outdoors to two art-filled sheds. Digging through piles to reveal shipwreck maps, celebrity posters, watercolors and wildlife paintings along the way for an adventure. At Ocean Gallery, shopping for art feels as creative as making it.

Phillip Morton Gallery
47 Baltimore Ave.302- 727-0905This gallery features 'fine art' in such media as sculpture, ceramics, mixed-media and painting with periodic exhibitions and private appointments available for viewing the collections. Shows and exhibitions are regularly on display.

SURF AND SKATE: GETTING BOARD

Alley-Oop Skim
2000 Coastal Hwy. Unit 106
Dewey Beach, DE
302-227-3622
Every year in early August, Dewey Beach hosts the East Coast Professional and ZAP! Amateur World Championship skimboarding competition. Alley-Oop's owner, Jason Wilson, is a world-ranking professional skim boarder whose father, Harry Wilson, founded this event in the early 80's. The shop offers gear, lessons and even camps from world-class skimboard professionals.

CONVERSATION: STEVE AND BARBARA CRANE
Browseabout Books

Since Steve and Barbara Crane opened Browseabout Books in 1975, the store has evolved from a small storefront to over 13,000 square feet of retail. In an industry where most independent booksellers have sadly shut their door, Browseabout is a celebrated success story and one of Rehoboth's retail treasures. Steve recounts how they do it.

"We were school teachers together in Wilmington, Barbara taught grades four through six and I was a phys ed teacher.

I grew up in a retail family, my father worked for Woolworth's and knew how to run a five-and-ten. He left the company when it re-organized and in 1964 he had the opportunity to run three stores in Stone Harbor, Avalon, and Ocean City. That was our first taste in the resort business.

I always wanted to do retail. We got the chance one summer, during the school vacation in the Rehoboth mini-mall. The store was very small. No telephone, no bathroom. Barbara always wanted to have a bookstore at the beach, and we also sold toys, candy, and tobacco. Barb taught one more year, I taught three.

The key to success in this business is being here. We come in every morning, make the coffee, process the sales, look at what we did the day before and which way we're going. We open at 6 a.m. seven days a week and close at 11 p.m. When we first started, Barbara stayed open until 2 a.m. She would ride a bicycle home with the receipts, the only thing she had to worry about were skunks going through the trash. The only time we took a loan was to put the café in.

We used to carry a bigger spectrum of books. There were more publishers and more titles. Now our stock is narrower. We try to draw off the cream. Our customers are on vacation; they're at the beach, so they read more fiction than non-fiction. Sixty per cent of our sales are books, people come in to buy a book and then maybe they pick up cards or something else.

The Internet has changed everything. In order to make an independent bookstore succeed, we have to give the customer a special experience.

My best idea was to utilize the outside of the store and make it as attractive as the inside. We had a local artist, Patty Shreve, paint books on the front and side of the street where people walking along the sidewalk can see them; we gave the titles a summer twist.

Rehoboth has always been a quality resort. The people who had the best jobs at their company would vacation in August, middle management came in July, and the guys starting out on the totem pole in June. That's changed. There are more people all year round now, there's more balance. ∎

East of Maui Surf Shop
104 St. Louis Street
Dewey Beach
302-227-4703
At the north side of Dewey, the surfboard-lined, Crayola-blue East of Maui surf shop provides proof-positive that this beach town is, indeed, a way of life. Stock includes kayaks, surf, skim, kite and paddleboards available for sale or rent. The pros at East of Maui can outfit every board sport adventure. Ask about lessons.

The Edge
28 Wilmington Ave.
302-227-2433
Going strong since the 90's, The Edge has been serving up the coolest surf and skate apparel on the corner of First Street and Wilmington Avenue from Day One. Window displays set in hollowed-out television sets set the hip tone. Alternative clothing, shoes, wallets, sunglasses and skate gear offered here is sure to make this shop is a must-stop for the skater boy or girl at the beach.

Quiet Storm
126 Rehoboth Avenue
302-226-2747
Part gear shop/part seaside outfitter, Quiet Storm offers big-name surf-styles and the boards to go with them. Contented beach bums stop here to pick up smart apparel for their laid-back lifestyle.

Rehoboth Beach Surf Shop
26 Wilmington Ave.
302-212-2619
A true surf-shack, this snug spot on Wilmington Avenue sells not only surf, skate and bodyboards but also offers rentals and lessons.

Woodrow sunglasses and long-sleeve hoodies complete the deal to transform land-loving sunbathers into surf riders.

Sierra Moon Surf & Skate
16 Rehoboth Avenue
302-227-3622
Sierra Moon has been a top spot to outfit body and skate boarders at the beach for almost as long as surfing and skating have been mainstream. Whether just starting out or well established in the pastimes, the sales team can set up customers with new gear and better threads. Expect better-than-average brands and friendly vibes from this surf-n-skate.

ON THE MOVE — BICYCLE SALES AND RENTALS

Atlantic Cycles
18 Wilmington Avenjue
302-226-2543
Located on the ocean block of Wilmington Avenue, Atlantic Cycles stocks a wide selection of bikes, surreys, tandems, cruisers, hybrids road bikes and bicycles for kids. Their brochure also includes an area map of downtown Rehoboth, so unfamiliar cyclists can get found before they get lost.

Bike To Go
174 Rehoboth Avenue
302-227-7600
This store has it all: repair shop, sales floor and an in-house inventory room filled with comfort cycles and hybrids available to rent by the hour, day or week.

SKIMBOARDING

Skimboarding, or skimming, is the lesser known of what seems to be a growing assortment of sports that operate via board. Surfboards, paddleboards, kiteboards and certainly skateboards got nothin' on the light, slender, typically wooden, fin-less skimboards that give riders a speedy glide to meet an oncoming, breaking wave and ride it back to shore. Wave-riding skimboarders can perform a number of wave maneuvers in various stages of their ride, including Big Spins and 360 Shuvs.

Unlike surfing, skimboarding begins on the beach, with riders dropping their board into the thin wash of previous waves, then using their momentum to skim out to breaking waves, do tricks, and catch a ride back to shore.

Bob's Rental

30 Maryland Avenue
302-227-7966
In more than 80 years at the same location, Bob's Bike Rental has been owned by only two families. These days, Bob's maintains the May 15-September 30 schedule that has worked for owner Bob Plunkett, Jr., and his family for the last 35 years. The shop offers a selection of nearly 400 bicycles available for rent, including the only red 11-seater limo surrey cycle available.

Seagreen Bicycle Rentals

54 Baltimore Avenue
302-226-2323
Recognizable by its selections of cobalt-blue cycles, surreys, joggers and trailers, Seagreen Bicycle Rentals has the newest fleet on the street. Located in a cedar-shingle building on the second block of Baltimore Avenue, Seagreen offers rentals, sales and repairs.

WHERE EVERYONE IS A KID: TOY STORES

Fun for All

42 Rehoboth Ave. (Penny Lane)
302-227-1015
This pint-sized toy store packs a ton of fun into a small space. Find more classic games and puzzles here along with everything from pinwheels to ant farms. A stock well suited to help pass rainy days.

Rehoboth Toy and Kite

1 Virginia Ave/67 Rehoboth Ave
302-226-5483/ 302-227-6996
If it's not the bubble machine working outside, then it's the mechanical toy puppies barking at the front door that welcomes you to this store and sets the tone for what's inside.

Sole Kids

110 Rehoboth Avenue
302-227-6622
Offspring of the ladies boutique next door, Sole Kids offers whimsical clothing and housewares for the youngest vacationers. Focused on the elementary school set and their younger siblings, Sole Kids carries kid-sized housewares and features board books as well as literature like "Everyone Poops." A floor-to-ceiling wall of classic toys will remind everyone of their younger years at this children's store.

GIFTS AND SPECIALTIES

Browseabout Books:

133 Rehoboth Ave.
302-226-2665
In an age of #hashtags and @twitter, Browseabout Books thrives because every trip inside is a reminder of why we need bookstores and reading that doesn't rely upon internet access or electricity. Management stocks the shelves with long-form narration, stationery, games and creative cards for the well-read set. A bookstore for book-lovers, Browseabout easily leads the literary pack with big-name book signings, charming cards, reliable recommendations and the best beach-reads.

Bella Luna

127 Rehoboth Avenue
302-227-0267
Bella Luna is the retail outlet of Janice Elder, a classically-trained artist who is apt to step down from her studio upstairs in the summer months with paint still on her hands and check on how sales associates are managing downstairs. The store is feminine and light-hearted, with objects of desire for the mind, body and soul around every corner.

Buddhas and Beads

232 Rehoboth Aveune
302-227-6004
This collectibles and antiques store specializes in estate jewelry, stones, precious metals and vintage musical instruments. An eclectic mix of art along with the Buddha statues— and beads— that give the store it's name. The owners are typically as happy to buy collectibles and precious metal, as they are to sell.

Christmas Spirit

161 Rehoboth Ave
302-227-6872
Looking for Christmas in July? Then this is the place to get set for celebrations. Long offering creative ornaments and holiday housewares, at this specialty shop, it really is Christmas year-round. No matter the season, here it's always the most wonderful time of the year.

Gidget's Gadgets

123 Rehoboth Avenue
302-227-4434

Part toy store, part novelties shop and all attitude, Gidget's Gadgets is always an interesting spot to stop. The store recently added a collection of vintage albums to the mix. Look for fun items like old-school toys, modern home furnishings, key chains and novelties directed at, or reminiscent of, your inner child.

Gifts of Serenity

42 Rehoboth Ave. (Penny Lane)
(302) 226-3691

Gifts of Serenity has been offering a wide variety of presents since 1985 to inspire tranquility. Best-selling items include Primal hand soaps, Crabtree and Evelyn skin care and Peace Frogs apparel.

Kitchy Stitch

413 Rehoboth Ave.
302-260-9138

The wall-art in this yarn store reminds shoppers to "Keep Calm and Knit On," but that might be easier said than done for knitting aficionados on vacation. Fortunately, in addition to a wide variety of yarn and a smallish collection of fabrics, store owner Allison Worthing hosts "Sit and Knit" parties open twice weekly to anyone with a knitting or crochet project, so knitters can spin a yarn while they spin their yarn.

Miss Pixie's by the Sea

40 Baltimore Ave/Rehoboth Mews
302-226- 8171

Although Miss Pixie's home furnishings is relatively new to the retail scene in Rehoboth, owner Pixie Windsor has a long history here. Once upon a time as a teenager, Miss Pixie sold taffy and popcorn at Dolle's. That was long before moving across the Chesapeake and opening her first location of Miss Pixies in NW Washington, D.C. Her new store is stocked with all the same types of artful items she picks up at auctions for her flagship store, but with a beachier feel. There's also complementary salt-water taffy for shoppers.

PROUD Bookstore

149 Rehoboth Ave. (Rehoboth Mews)
302-227-6969

With it's rainbow-colored logo, PROUD bookstore is a specialty shop that concentrates on offering literature, gifts and accessories for a clientele that is out, and about. LBGT news and reading.

Ryan's Gems and Junk

(and rooftop mini golf!)
1 Delaware Avenue
302-227-3797

Ryan's Beach Store, AKA Ryan's Gem's and Junk, opened in 1961 and still embodies the beach experience. Located on the boardwalk near Delaware Avenue, Ryan's is a one-stop shop for the sun and sand, selling hermit crabs, sunscreen, beach toys and sundries. Be sure to stop upstairs to play a round of golf with a view at the only mini-golf course in downtown Rehoboth, located on the roof.

Sea Shell Shop

119 Rehoboth Avenue
302-227-6666

With a nautical focus and singular theme, the sea shell shop has been supplying household accessories, decorative pieces, and souvenirs since the 1970s.

Superkind

157 Rehoboth Avenue
302-226-0800

Superkind doesn't resemble most Rehoboth retailers with its distinctive storefront and entrance. Owner Tim Duffy displays a collection of satirical stickers and witticisms along the walkways that make his steps seem like a stairway to heaven for shoppers who walk to beat of their own drum. Inside, find whatever dead-headed threads or artsy Guatemalan ponchos have caught Duffy's fancy that season along with a selection of vintage vinyl, stickers, jewelry and tapestries that made the cut.

Something Comfortable

122 Rehoboth Avenue
302-227-6810

This tasteful lingerie boutique caters to parties. Whether they be bachelorette parties or a girls night out, pre-arranged parties Something Comfortable promises to keep the fun flowing and the party going with plenty of lingerie and undergarment options that look good and feel better.

LIVING LOCAL
Attractions & Listings

ATTRACTIONS

JUNGLE JIM'S:

With waterslides, bumper boats, go-karts, miniature golf, batting cages, and rock climbing this is a great family break from the beach. $35 admission per person (reduced Twilight rates).
8 Country Club Rd., 302-227-8444

MOVIES AT MIDWAY:

The closest movie theater to Rehoboth with multiple screens offers a comfortable if homey setting (no glitz or glamour but $1 candy). All-day schedule makes for convenience and choice.
Route 1, Midway Shopping Center;
302-645-0200

RYAN'S MINI GOLF: ON THE BOARDWALK

Minature golf above the boardwalk with an ocean view for $4. Course is well-kept if simple (no obstacles or moving objects) but it's the rooftop location that makes it special. Reviewers call it 'one of the most enjoyable and inexpensive family opportunities in town.'

MIDWAY SPEEDWAY PARK

Go-carts and mini-golf. Some visitors have a blast and return every year for an annual pit stop, others report a different experience.
18645 Coastal Hwy., (302) 644-2042

JOLLY TROLLEY OF REHOBOTH BEACH

Even if vacation plans don't yet include a trip to Dewey Beach, no holiday in Rehoboth is complete without a ride on the Jolly Trolley.

Since 1970, the Jolly Trolley has operated a mass transit system from Rehoboth to Dewey Beach. With stops along the way, this shuttle service transports thousands of cheerful commuters from one seaside town to the next. For just a few dollars, friendly trolley drivers give travellers a chance to keep their cars parked and sit back to relax as passengers, beating the traffic and prevailing over the inconveniences of parking.

A family-owned and operated business, the Jolly Trolley runs a regular route from 8 a.m. to 2 a.m., Memorial Day through Labor Day with abbreviated hours through the shoulder seasons. Not only does the Jolly Trolley now offer private charters with a variety of vehicles, the company has also teamed up with the Rehoboth Beach Museum for illuminating Jolly Trolley history tours. At the Anna Hazzard tent house (17 Christian Street), a local historian brings to life the Reverend Robert W. Todd, the Methodist minister credited with founding Rehoboth Beach, as riders sit back for a revealing oration about the history of this beach town.

In the summer months, the Jolly Trolley runs regular shuttles from Rehoboth to Dewey Beach every half hour (even more often at peak times). Reservations are required for the Jolly Trolley History Tours. For more information or reservations, call 302-227-7310. ∎

CALENDAR OF EVENTS

SEASONAL

Polar Bear Plunge Festival (February) is for the 'bears' who dare to dive in to the water and the less brave types who get to sample the food and spectacle, all for to benefit Special Olympics Delaware.

Designer Show House (May) benefits the Village Improvement Association and demonstrates how to transform an ordinary house into a drop-dead gorgeous interior and landscape. www.rehobothbeachvia.org

Greyhounds 'Reach the Beach' (April, October) brings throngs of greyhounds (and the folks who love them). Quite a sight throughout town as dozens of these stunning animals take their humans out for a walk. greyhoundevents.com/

Rehoboth Beach Farmer's Market (May-October) on Tuesday, noon-4 pm (after October 1, noon-3) in Grove Park, rain or shine. 25 vendors selling vegetables, fruit, cheese, meat, seafood, prepared food, baked goods, plants and cut flowers. www.rbfarmersmarket.com

Restaurant Week (June) offers affordable ($25-45) three course prix-fixe meals at many of the town's best restaurants.

Rehoboth Beach Bandstand (throughout the season) hosts live family entertainment and movies. Program schedule www.rehobothbandstand.com/

Delaware Seashore State Park Pontoon Boat Tours (throughout the season) from the dock at Indian River Marina explore the inland bays. Morning trips are 'hands on', the afternoon trip is pure enjoyment—both are appropriately 'ecology-heavy'. Limited seating, pre-registration strongly recommended. 302-227-6991 destateparks.com/park/delaware-seashore/programs/index.asp

Cottage Tour of Art (July) to benefit the Art League invites visitors into a half-dozen private homes as well as the Homestead on the League grounds. www.rehoboth-artleague.org

Independence Day Fireworks (July 4) have become a thing of local pride as Rehoboth Beach Main Street provides a full Zambelli Internationale spectacle over the Atlantic.

Dewey Beach Running of the Bull (mid-July) is the Cape's closest thing to Hemingway's Pamplona. The costumed 'bull' may be less than frightening but the massive crew of party-ready 'participants' is still death defying.

Rehoboth Art League Outdoor Show

(August) hosted over two week-ends features selected artists from the Mid-Atlantic region. Now in its fourth decade, the setting itself in the sylvan glen of the League grounds is itself landscape art. www.rehoboth-artleague.org

Polish Festival Polkamotion by the Ocean

(mid-September) packs the town from Thursday through Sunday. All the polka, beer, sausage and galumpkis you can pack into one weekend, wrapping up with Sunday Mass at the convention center.

Coast Day

(October) at University of Delaware Hugh R. Sharp Campus, 700 Pilottown, Lewes is a celebration and introduction to Delaware's wonders of the sea. Visitors can interact with researchers, tour ships, try hands-on activities and attend presentations. Live music, vendor displays, and seafood favorites chosen from the Crab Cake Cook-Off and the Seafood Chowder Challenge. University of Delaware Environmental Public Education Office at 302-831-8083, DeCoastDay@udel.edu.

Rehoboth Beach Jazz Festival

(October) brings big talent jazz performers to town for an extended October week-end that puts Rehoboth on the music map (who woulda' thought!). Multiple sites, including the 'acoustically perfect' auditorium at Cape Henlopen High School. www.rehobothjazz.com

Sea Witch Halloween and Fiddler's Festival

Reaching back into the late 1980's, Rehoboth was still an extremely seasonal town where many businesses were forced to close in the winter due to a lack of activity in tourism. That only lasted until Carol Everhart, president and CEO of the Rehoboth-Dewey Beach chamber of Commerce brought her brainchild, the first-ever Sea Witch Halloween and Fiddler's Festival to Rehoboth in 1989.

Far from an extreme fear-fest, Everhart created an event to capture the feeling of the autumn and bring visitors back to town. Held the weekend before Halloween each year, the Sea Witch Festival includes seasonal decorations, games, scarecrow stuffing and parades in this downtown costume party.

These days, the Sea Witch Festival includes a steady schedule of performances on the bandstand including the annual fiddler's contest, beach games for kids, a 5K run-walk, two parades (one for pets), pony and hayrides.

www.beach-fun.com/
Rehoboth-Dewey Chamber
of Commerce site

courtesy of Portraits In the Sand

LIVING Local

Punkin' Chunkin (October) is a Sussex County good time at its 'most Sussex County-est' when engineering innovation combines with pure human whimsy to see who can launch a pumpkin furthest. This unlikely sporting event was invented locally and now gets international TV coverage. www.punkinchunkin.com/

Rehoboth Beach Independent Film Festival (November) features a five-day showcase of approximately 100 American and international films including features, documentaries, and shorts. www.rehobothfilm.com/festival.html

Downtown Holiday Tree Lighting and Sing-a-Long (December) is an annual holiday tradition, complete with the opening of Santa's House on the Boardwalk. 302-227-2772, www.downtownrehoboth.com/

Rehoboth Beach Main Street organizes a spectrum of events to promote downtown including a Mardi Gras & Gumbo Cook-Off and a Spring Chocolate Festival. www.downtownrehoboth.com

Annual Fall (October) and Spring (May) Sidewalk Sales where merchants purge stock at huge discounts, dealers display collectibles and 'yard sale' types empty attics. Chamber of Commerce (302) 227–6446 or www.beach-fun.com

YEAR-LONG

Cape Henlopen State Park offers a variety of programs and special activities. For more information, call the Seaside Nature Center at 302-645-6852; www.destateparks.com

Rehoboth Art League offers a variety of classes and events for adults and children. For information call 302-227-8408; www.rehobothartleague.org

Osher Lifelong Learning at the Lewes division of the University of Delaware is available to all learners age 50 and older. Classes are held at various locations in Rehoboth Beach and Lewes. Catalog and registration forms available online at www.lifelonglearning.udel.edu/lewes 302-645- 4111

Rehoboth Beach Public Library, Story Time for Tots and Pre-Schoolers Ages 1-3, Wednesdays, 10:30 am; Ages 4-5, Mondays, 11:00 am. 226 Rehoboth Avenue, 302-227-8044

Performing Arts Classes hosted by Clear Space Theatre Company. Information at www.clearspaceproductions.org

Rehoboth Beach Writers offers a variety of writing workshops, readings, and special events. www.rehobothbeachwritersguild.com/

The Rehoboth Beach Chamber of Commerce maintains an extensive, ongoing listing of events to be found at http www.rehoboth.com (Events & Activities).

Wibergart Gallery

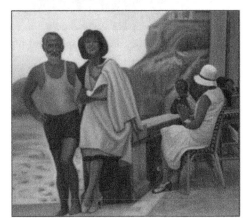

Gallery 50

Amadeline Gallery

'SECOND SATURDAY' MOSAIC ART WALK

Mosaic, the Rehoboth Beach Gallery Collective organized in 2007 by some dozen galleries, showcases the local scene on the second Saturday evening of each month when they open their doors downtown for a celebration 'Art Walk' from 6:00 to 9:00 pm.

"A symbolic welcome mat into the world of visual art for the entire community," is how the organizers describe the year-round event. "A time when anyone can mingle with visual artists, discuss the art making process, chat with gallery owners, and enjoy a culinary treat."

Their Facebook page, MosaicRehoboth, posts information announcements, as well as links that show what each of the galleries will be displaying that evening.

Among Participating Galleries are:
- Heidi Lowe
  (328 Rehoboth Avenue, 302-227-9203)
- Kevin Flemming and Friends
  (239 Rehoboth Avenue, 302-227-4994)
- Philip Morton Gallery
  (47 Baltimore Avenue, 302-727-0905)
- Ward Ellinger Gallery
  (39 Baltimore Avenue, 302-227-2710)
- Paintiques
  (20 Baltimore Avenue, 302-258-4203)
- Wibergart Gallery
  (20 Baltimore Avenue, 302-245-3615)
- Amandeline
  (20 Baltimore Avenue, 302-226-0330)
- Juleez Art
  (N 1st Street, 302-227-3792)
- Gallery 50
  (50 B Wilmington Avenue, 302-227-2050)

ANNUAL NANTICOKE INDIAN POWWOW

Powwow, from the Narragansett Eastern Algonquian language, is any gathering of native people. The Nanticoke define their three-day powwow as a cultural event with group singing and dancing to pass traditions from generation to generation. Each powwow begins with a Grand Entry or procession of dancers serving as the "bringing together of tribes." Dancers enter the dance circle by age and style of regalia.

"We gathered on the dusty trail at the edge of the woods and jumped aboard two bench seats pulled by a tractor," reported one spectator. "I enjoyed the bumpy ride into the forest and the warm breezes on my face. Immediately the sounds and rhythm of the drums captured my senses. I felt dwarfed by the ancient trees and walked with respect for I knew I was on sacred ground."

Native arts and crafts including jewelry, pottery, moccasins, ribbon shirts, shawls, dream catchers, and paintings are on display and offered for sale. ■

Usually the first weekend after Labor Day 26800 John J. Williams Highway, Millsboro, Delaware 19966. Nanticoke Indian Museum, 302-945-7022; www.nanticokeindians.org

ANNA HAZZARD MUSEUM

Rehoboth's last remaining one room 'tent house' dating from the town's origins as a Methodist camp-meeting, this museum reflects the era through artifacts and memorabilia.

It is named in honor of former owner Anna Hazzard, the first woman to receive a real estate broker's license in Delaware (1902). She would go on to become Secretary of the Women's Christian Temperance Union and President of the Rehoboth Art League. ■

*17 Christian Street
302-226-1119*

CAPE MAY TO LEWES FERRY

Residents have long taken advantage of the Cape May to Lewes Ferry to avoid the long driving detour around the state of Delaware, thus shaving hours from their trip (and also reducing their carbon footprint in the process). But one of the best-kept local secrets is that the Ferry also makes a great day trip for Rehoboth visitors who want to savor the 'lure of the sea' for a couple of hours of a quick get-away.

The 80-minute ride on one of four state-of-the-art motor vessels provides a wonderful opportunity to sit back, relax and enjoy the 17-mile journey in style. En route, passengers get a front row seat to some of the most spectacular views of Cape Henlopen and the Delaware Bay.

The Delaware ferry terminal is located on Route 9 in Lewes Delaware, a short 15- minute ride from downtown Rehoboth (but be aware of travel delays on Route 1 in season). The New Jersey terminal connects with the Garden State Parkway for easy transit to all points north.

Soon after leaving the terminal at Lewes, there is a stunning close-up of the red and black-banded Breakwater East End Lighthouse. The Harbor of Refuge Lighthouse is just a short distance away as you head past the breakwater for Cape May and its own imposing lighthouse. You may also see pods of dolphins racing ahead of the bow wave along with the occasional Right whale migrating off the coast of Delaware Bay.

The ferries depart every hour to hour-and-a-half from April to October but check the web site as schedules and frequency change. Fares for car and driver during peak season (Memorial Day to Labor Day) are $45 one-way. Foot passengers pay $10 ($8 seniors) one-way and kids under 6 are free. Shuttle Service is provided from Rehoboth Beach by DART to the Park and Ride lot where the Ferry Shuttle takes you to the Lewes Ferry Terminal ($4, children under 6 free). ∎

See capemaylewesferry.com for full details regarding ferry operations and events.

SURVIVAL GUIDE

GETTING TO REHOBOTH

BY CAR

Directions From Washington DC & Baltimore, Maryland:
Take Route 50 East over the Chesapeake Bay Bridge. Follow Route 50 after the bridge. Take a left onto Route 404 East. Continue on 404 East. At the circle in Georgetown, Delaware, take Route 9 East. Turn right onto Route 1 South. Get in your left-hand lane on Route 1 South. Follow Exit 1-A (on the left) for Rehoboth Beach Avenue Access.

Directions From Philadelphia, Pennsylvania & New Jersey:
Take 95 South through Wilmington, DE and take exit 4A (Route 1 South toward Dover). Continue through Dover, Milford, and Lewes. Get in your left-hand lane on Route 1 South. Follow Exit 1-A (on the left) for Rehoboth Beach Avenue Access.

Directions From Cape May/ Lewes Ferry in Lewes, Delaware:
Turn right onto Cape Henlopen Drive (west). Turn left onto Kings Highway/US 9. Turn left onto Route 1 South. Get in your left-hand lane on Route 1 South. Follow Exit 1-A (on the left) for Rehoboth Beach Avenue Access.

Directions From the South:
Take Route 1 North toward Delaware. Continue through Fenwick Island, Bethany Beach, and Dewey Beach. Stay straight onto DE-1 ALT North. DE-1 ALT becomes 2nd Street. Make a right on Rehoboth Avenue to continue on toward the Boardwalk.

BY BUS

Greyhound (www.greyhound.com or call 1-800-454-2487): Service to Ocean City, Maryland. From there you can contact shuttle or limousine services listed below.

DART First State (800-652-3278): Between Rehoboth Beach and Wilmington www.dartfirststate.com

DC2NY (a Washington-based bus company) offers service from DuPont Circle in Washington, DC, to Rehoboth Beach and Dewey Beach from Friday through Monday during the summer. To view a schedule and rate structure, visit www.DC2NY.com.

DC2NY also offers Rehoboth Beach service from Wilmington and New York (Penn Station at 33rd Street and Seventh Avenue).

BY AIR

AREA & REGIONAL AIRPORTS

Georgetown, DE, Air Services:
302-855-2355
Private planes only. 25 minutes from Rehoboth Beach.

New Castle County, DE, Airport:
302-571-6474
Private planes only. 1:45 minutes from Rehoboth Beach.

Philadelphia, PA, International Airport:
2 hours from Rehoboth Beach.

Salisbury-Ocean City, MD Regional Airport: 410-548-4827
5 minutes from Rehoboth Beach.

Baltimore-Washington International Airport (BWI):
2 hours from Rehoboth Beach

Reagan National Airport (DC):
2 hours from Rehoboth Beach.

BY TRAIN

Amtrak services Delaware from New York to Washington, stopping at Wilmington, Delaware.

SOUTH END OF BOARD WALK AND PLAYLAND, REHOBOTH BEACH, DEL.

From there one can hire a car service or take a DART bus from Wilmington for $7.50 one way (from Memorial Day through Labor Day buses from the Amtrak station). www.dart-firststate.com/information/programs/beach-bus/

LIMO SERVICES

ASA Transportation and Airport Shuttle
(302-698-3555)
Transportation locally and airport/train connections;

Atlantic Transportation Services
(302-644-6999)
Chauffeured transport for one to 27 passengers.

VISITORS INFORMATION:

HISTORIC REHOBOTH RAILROAD STATION
502 Rehoboth Avenue, 302-227-2233
The Rehoboth railroad station built in 1879, originally located at the foot of Rehoboth Avenue at the boardwalk, now stands at 502 Rehoboth Avenue (as you enter town) and serves as the Chamber of Commerce Visitor's Information Center. The building has been restored, with vintage details and photographs. One visitor calls it "a nice little haven for pulling safely out of traffic and re-grouping, with the added value of its setting in a woodsy little park."

PARKING

Parking meters are in effect from the Friday before Memorial Day through the second Sunday following Labor Day, from 10 am until midnight.

Meter Rates are $1.50/hr. and may be paid in quarters (see below) or by credit card via Parkmobile (download the free mobile app at www.parkmobile.com or call 1-877-727-5758) All 30-minute parking spaces are $2.00/hr. and are time limited the entire year.

All non-metered areas of the city require a parking permit

Persons driving vehicles with a handicap plate or permit are required to pay for parking meters and parking permits while they are in effect.

LIVING Local

Vehicle Parking Permit Information

Parking permits are required in all non-metered areas within the city and are in effect from the Friday before Memorial Day through Labor Day, 10 am – 5 pm. Parking permits are NOT valid for metered parking spots.

Permits can be purchased at the following locations:

Rehoboth Avenue and Bayard Avenue (Satellite locations);
Parking Meter Division (30.5 Lake Avenue, behind City Hall, 302-227-6184);
Select real estate offices at check-in;
Visitors Center (501 Rehoboth Avenue).

Permit Prices:

Seasonal Non-transferable - $175
Effective August 1 - $88
Seasonal Transferable - $200
Effective August 1 - $100
Weekly - $45
Three Day Weekend - $30
Weekend Daily (Saturday, Sunday) - $13
Weekday Daily (Monday - Friday) - $8

SMOKE FREE AREAS

The City of Rehoboth Beach adopted a new ordinance that prohibits the smoking of tobacco products — including cigarettes, cigars and pipes — in specified areas within the city, effective May 15, 2014. Prohibited areas include:

- The Boardwalk and Accessways;
- The Beach and Dune Crossings;
- The Bandstand Plaza;
- City Parks and Children's Playgrounds;

PUBLIC LIBRARY

Rehoboth Beach Library
226 Rehoboth Ave.(302) 227-8641
Hours: Monday thru Wednesday
10:00 am - 8:00 pm
Thursday & Friday
10:00 am - 8:00 pm
Saturday 10:00 am - 3:00 pm
Sunday 12:00 pm - 4:00 pm

POST OFFICE

Rehoboth Beach Post Office,
179 Rehoboth Avenue, (302)227-8241
Monday-Friday 9:00 a.m. - 5:00 p.m.
Saturday 8:30 a.m.-12:30 p.m.

21—Beach, Boardwalk, and Cottage Line looking North, Rehoboth Beach, Delaware

EMERGENCIES (Call 911)

Police and Fire
Rehoboth Beach Police Department:
(302) 227-2577
Dewey Beach Police Department:
(302) 227-1110
State Police, Troop 7 (Lewes):
(302) 644-5020
Rehoboth Volunteer Fire Company:
(302) 227-8400

Hospitals and Emergency Centers
Beebe Healthcare (General Hospital):
424 Savannah Road, Lewes;
(302) 645-3300;
Beebe Emergency Room: (302) 645-3291

Emergency Veterinarians
Savannah Animal Hospital,
33818 Wescoats Road, Lewes DE 19958;
(302)645-8757; 24 hour emergency service
for clients and non-clients;

'WHAT'S HAPPENING': BLOGS, SITES & TWEETS

Cape Gazette, the newspaper of record on the Cape since its founding in 1993, posts a daily update of news, events, and local happenings. www.capegazette.villagesoup.com

Rehoboth Beach Chamber of Commerce, the definitive calendar of events. www.rehoboth.com/events-a-activities

The Rehoboth Foodie. The ultimate insider on restaurants and restaurateurs. http://www.rehobothfoodie.com/

About My Beaches: Life along the Delmarva coast from charities to restaurants to farmer's markets. www.aboutmybeaches.com:

Rehoboth Real Estate: Area information, resources and listings viewed through the perspective of one of Rehoboth Beach's leading realtors. www.rehobothrealestate.com

Locals Only: Hadley McGregor's curated postings of local purveyors of everything from A (art) to W (weddings). www.localsonlyunderground.com

Rehoboth Beach Fever: Liz Marie has been coming to Rehoboth Beach for over twenty years and shares her tips with other vacationers on where to stay and what to do. www.rehobothbeachfever.com

ACKNOWLEDGEMENTS

Revealing Rehoboth is the product of lots of insiders, all of whom deserve great thanks.

The inspiration for the book---its 'muse' as she jokingly calls herself---is Susan McAnelly, the extraordinary 'major domo' at Browseabout Books in Rehoboth Beach. It was Susan who kept urging us to produce a guide to Rehoboth like the one we did for Lewes, *Living Lewes*. This book wouldn't have happened without her enthusiasm and support. Ditto Alex Colevas, another great early ally at Browseabout.

The Rehoboth Beach Historical Society is lucky, indeed, to have Nancy Alexander as its Director and head honcho of the Rehoboth Beach Museum. She and her colleagues continue to assemble and display an ever-expanding material portrait of the town's past, including the recollections of assorted citizens in a wonderful set of oral histories. Her help has been invaluable.

In writing this book, I have been consistently impressed with the quality of Rehoboth Beach's cultural and civic organizations. The love (and gratitude) so many feel toward this community is clear. I spoke with leaders of many of these groups and want to thank them for sharing with me their ambitious visions: Chris Bason (Delaware Center for the Inland Bays), Sheila Bravo (The Rehoboth Art League), Sue Early (Rehoboth Film Society), Steve Elkins (CAMP Rehoboth), Denise Emery (Coastal Concerts), Dennis Santangini (Delaware Celebration of Jazz), and Doug Yetter (Clear Space Theater). Longtime Mayor Sam Cooper educated me on the doings of his office.

Rich Barnett, a deft writer, gave of his talent willingly and graciously.

My cohorts in the Mulberry Street Collective are a special bunch. Molly MacMillan, co-author, contributed her vitality, creativity and non-stop enthusiasm. Rob Sturgeon showed up just when he was most needed. Not only does Bob Yesbek know about food, as a writer he's a consummate professional. Howard Hundley is our fisherman *extraordinaire*.

About Design Director Rob Waters, I can only repeat what I often say to anyone who will listen: "This is one very serious talent!"

As always and with every project I undertake, the biggest 'thank you' goes to wife Catherine Clarke. She's the base from which all good things stem.

Neil Shister

CPSIA information can be obtained at www.ICGtesting.com
Printed in the USA
BVOW10s1628131214

379250BV00003B/3/P